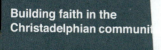

TIDINGS

Volume 86, Number 9 / October, 2023

IN THIS ISSUE

Editorial—Exchanging Comfort for Growth, **Dave Jennings** 2
 —Racism and Clans, **a Brother**...........................8
 —Cast Your Net on the Other Side, **Matthew Blewett**..........10
Life Application—Anger, **Jonathan Farrar**........................16
Prayer—Praying on Behalf of Others, **Shawn Moynihan** 22
Exhortation and Consolation—Technology and the Ecclesia,
 Jonathan Schwieger.................32
Music and Praise—Energy, Unity and Creativity, **Jessica Gelineau** 37
 —Worldwide Praise, Worship and Bible Study, **Simon Tarypally** . .43
Bible Studies — Words I Hope I Never Hear Again (2), **David Levin** 46
 —Getting to Know our God and Jesus, **Jim Styles**............51
First Principles —Preaching First Principles in a Post-Christian World,
 Richard Morgan 56
Book Review—*Starters*, reviewed by **Mike Hardy** 61
Notice—New Worship Book, **Rachel Hocking** 62
Preaching and Teaching—Good Morning Vietnam!, **Alan Ghent** 63
 —St. Lucia and St. Vincent, **Mike LeDuke**...................68
 —A Baptism in Quito, **Kevin Hunter** 70

WHY are most ecclesias in North America predominantly white and middle-class? Only some of our ecclesias match the racial demographics of the communities where we worship. This situation is not unique to Christadelphia. Recent surveys have found that while 85% of all Christian churches desire greater diversity, less than 15% have realized that goal.[1] Men and women commonly congregate with those most like themselves. I suppose this makes sense. We tend to find more comfort with those with similar interests, common concerns and those at the same relative economic level. In America, cities and suburbs often formed along similar ethnic and economic boundaries.

Yet the gospel calls for us to embrace quite a different viewpoint than our cultural norm in society. The very gospel message spoken to Abraham was that through Abraham and his Seed, "shall all nations be blessed." (Gal 3:8). In Christ, all distinctions are erased. *"There is neither Jew nor Greek, there is neither bond nor free, there is neither male nor female: for ye are all one on Christ Jesus."* (Gal 3:28). God always intended to redeem faithful men and women of all nations, cultures and languages. In many ways, this was the purpose of the spirit gifts at Pentecost.

Racial segregation in worship is not new. At the time of the apostles, we read of a synagogue in Jerusalem organized around an ethnic enclave of freed slaves from Cyrene, Alexandria, Cilicia, and the province of Asia (Acts 6:9). There was an unhelpful distinction between Grecian and Hebraic widows. One of the early challenges to the infant church was finding unity in a dynamic, growing body where each preaching campaign added more diversity. As the church grew, many Jewish believers grew increasingly frustrated with the challenges of diversity. Some even wanted to resist change by imposing the culture and practices of Judaism on Gentile believers. While all believers rejoiced in the Gentile reception of the gospel, they were unwilling to accept that their manner of worship and religious traditions should be subject to change. Theirs was a mindset of assimilation, not integration.

But is This What the Gospel Calls for in Ecclesias?

We do see ethnic and cultural diversity in our community when we look globally. Today our community is truly made up of faithful people from all countries and of every language and culture. We rejoice over this. What we don't often see is integration within ecclesias. Not surprisingly, the same phenomenon of homogeneity is common among most North American church denominations, and there is plenty of literature to read on this topic. Most congregations struggle to realize ethnic and cultural diversity. As one author put it,

> I don't think Christians have intentionally tried to remain culturally and racially divided, but the challenges of fellowshipping in an integrated church are significant. Ultimately, it is simply much easier to divide into our own comfortable groups, and form churches where people agree with

each other about doctrine, and want to worship and practice the same way. The effort that it takes to understand cultural differences is, for many people, simply not worth the potential return. In the end, church segregation happens, not purely by intent, **but because people do not actively work against it.**[2]

In the US business world, companies have struggled to increase ethnic diversity for decades. They created programs to "affirmatively" include more racial diversity in companies. Having been part of the management of such programs, I can attest that these efforts clearly had some value. However, over the years, companies learned that simple racial "representation" was never enough. The goal was to achieve a competitive value in diversity, using their diversity as a strategy in the marketplace. For example, having more diversity in a marketing group provides improved consumer insights. The aim of the best companies was not to force ethnic hires but to seek diversity as a tool to make their company stronger. Companies sought diversity because it made them better.

When it comes to the value of integration in Christian congregations, one author said it this way:

> One reason I want to see racial reconciliation, multi-ethnic congregations, and greater diversity among evangelicals is because I want more of the Bible. **And every time I get to know people from other cultures and backgrounds, my Bible grows.** I see new things. I get new angles into the truth of God's inspired Word. I find new treasures.[3]

Christadelphians should have a special appreciation of this principle, being a lay clergy. Hearing the gospel expounded by a wide swath of brethren gives us insights we often would not have had. When we hear an exhortation from a brother who has endured the loss of a job or gone through a serious health scare, we can get insights, even if we haven't personally had that experience. Add to these insights based on varied ages and experiences or from those who have come from outside the community, and we get alternative ways to understand the messages of the Bible. The more inclusive we are, the richer our examination and comprehension of the Scriptures.

Learning From Other Regions

I re-read a fascinating article by Bro. Craig Blewett on the radical change to preaching in South Africa. We're re-publishing his article in this issue for your consideration. The South African ecclesias entered this century with a recognition they needed to do something substantial if their ecclesias were to survive. They tried to reach the Black community by employing traditional preaching with conventional strategies. But they obtained poor results. As Bro. Craig described it,

> Little emphasis was placed on developing long-term relationships with target communities and welfare was typically limited to

members of our own community. Consequently, we scarcely reflected the diversity of the South African population, or the transformation being experienced throughout the country.[4]

Something urgently needed to change. Finally, a brother challenged the ecclesias to think out of the box—to consider transformational change. This activity took the form of "Good News Centers" in communities characterized by a history of racial mistrust following Apartheid. They soon found that developing relationships through "touching communities" (direct involvement in real, tangible works) helped turn stony soil into fertile land. They created preschools for children (aged two to five); they developed several feeding programs, provided after-school homework and support classes, provided artisanal (craft) workshops, organized gatherings for older women, and started sports programs. These activities met real community needs and allowed ecclesial members to find many ways to contribute.

These changes led to improved relationships. Improved relationships led to discussions about the Scriptures. Those discussions led to baptisms. In the September *Tidings* issue, we communicated a need for funding for the South African Bible School. That Bible School now draws heavily from disadvantaged communities and a racially integrated school, as are many ecclesias now in South Africa.

We would be wise in North American ecclesias to learn from our South African brothers and sisters. It may be that the specific programs implemented in their country aren't an exact match for us in North America. However, they learned that repeatedly doing the same things did not provide different

results. When they developed trusting relationships in communities where they previously had little presence, their preaching efforts found a more effective and sustainable seedbed.

We have also seen a revival in many UK ecclesias in recent years. They, too, were experiencing diminishing numbers, and some ecclesias closed. Then, the LORD blessed them with a remarkable influx of Iranian refugees. These refugees were seeking a Christian church and the Christadelphian unique unitarian doctrine drew them. The integration of new Iranian brothers and sisters has led these ecclesias to make fundamental changes in their worship services, and they have redirected much more of their energy into teaching first principles and nurturing new disciples. This development substantially changed the weekly experience of a member in one of these ecclesias. Diversity increased membership but required thoughtful and reasonable accommodations outside normal comfort areas.

In 2020, Bro. Steven Cox wrote this:

> A term frequently discussed is 'integration,' which is sometimes misunderstood by those on the periphery of the changes in the UK to mean Iranians must learn English. For those in ecclesias which are now majority Iranian on Sunday mornings they know that 'integration' is a two-way street.[5]

Working to become a multicultural community in North America will likely require difficult adjustments and sensitive discussions. If we wish to integrate differences, not assimilate, then we must be firm on first principle doctrinal issues but flexible on cultural matters. For example, how we demonstrate joy and express praise may differ from one culture to another. Are we willing to embrace alternative practices? The gospel compels us to change. Integration demands change. The status quo we are accustomed to is predictable and comfortable, but it comes at a great cost.

For Your Consideration

This editorial offers no answers. Rather, it is a call for all ecclesias to seriously consider why our ecclesial halls so rarely reflect the ethnicity of the neighborhoods we worship in. That assessment should include a look at our willingness to change and the value we place on having racially and culturally integrated ecclesias. Ultimately, we are responsible for the realities we see in front of us. Assuming we do want ecclesias to embrace ethnic and cultural diversity, what practices might inhibit integration? Do we preach in our own or disadvantaged areas? Would we consider adapting our worship services if required? Are we preaching to a community with which we have little to no relationship? Is our message addressing the needs of the neighborhood around us?

Let me give you an example. If our ecclesial hall is located in a low-income neighborhood (frequently the case), crime and social injustice are often real problems for those living there. What should our preaching message be to that community? Should we expound on Bible prophecy, describing how we believe the Last Days will unfold? Or should we address how Jesus will radically change the world at his

Editorial / Exchanging Comfort for Growth

return? How does God care for the disadvantaged? How will the Kingdom ensure justice for all? Jesus spoke to crowds that the Jewish religious leaders were abusing. He offered them the vision of living immediately in the Kingdom of Heaven, repentance, forgiveness and grace. His words resonated with them, and he met them right where they were.

Isolation, whether intended or unintended, is not the model of our Lord. His work was often with the poor, the sick and the diseased, and those feeling dispossessed. His preaching addressed their concerns and lifted them from despair. Jesus knew the value of worshipping with all people. New disciples came from within the towns and hamlets of Israel—often on the streets and in unpleasant settings. We know little change happened at that time inside the more sterile synagogue precincts.

To win people for Christ, the Apostle Paul changed himself, his message and his practices. (1 Cor 9:21-23). The NLT makes the commitment even more clear:

> When I am with those who are weak, I share their weakness, for I want to bring the weak to Christ. Yes, I try to find common ground with everyone, doing what I can to save some. I do everything to spread the Good News and share its blessings. (1 Cor 9:22-23 NLT).

In 1969, Bro. John Bilello authored an important article about racial prejudice, published in The *Christadelphian Magazine*. He rightly concluded that our community has much work to do to better integrate.

> Prejudice cannot abound if true brotherly love exists. Likewise, our claim of love for Father and Son, whom we have yet to behold, will fall on deaf ears in that day if we cannot unreservedly love our brother whom we have seen. For we know that His Kingdom will be based on a divine constitution which will cast away for ever the prejudices of man and the men who possessed them.[6]

At the end of the day, it all comes down to us as individuals. Are we willing to change? Will we exchange comfort and predictability for growth? Are we just another white church in North America? Or will we be a *"house of prayer for all people."* (Isa 56:7).

Dave Jennings

---

[1] All Smietana, Bob, *Racial Diversity at Church More Dream Than Reality*, Lifeway Research, January 17, 2014.
[2] Zimmerman, Jacob, *Moving Toward Racially and Culturally Integrated Churches*, Christian Perspectives: Society and Life, November 3, 2019.
[3] Wax, Trevin, *I Want a Bigger Bible*, August 13, 2015, The Gospel Coalition.
[4] Blewett, Craig, *South Africa: Cast Your Net on the Other Side*, The Christadelphian Tidings, June 30, 2020.
[5] Cox, Steven, *The Iranian Émigré Community (UK)*, The Christadelphian Tidings, June 30, 2020.
[6] Bilello, John C., *Racial Prejudice Examined in Light of the Scriptures*, The Christadelphian, Vol. 109, 1969.

RACISM AND CLANS

By a Brother

WE are clannish as humans. We feel devoted to our group, however defined, and we tend to care for those in our perceived group. The "clan" we initially embrace is the nuclear family. We expand in small increments to include more distant family members and then friends and schoolmates. Still, we tend to be very stingy about those we include in our "clans." That's the issue, that stinginess. We craft or create our clan, and our devotion is primarily to them.

In Christ, on the other hand, our essential relation to people is defined by "Thou shalt love thy neighbor as thyself," (Matt 22:39), and we see the entirety of Scripture as an illustration of that point. Scripture says we don't get to choose those we love and tend to. Every boundary we create, each limit we craft, negates the teaching. Still, our actions always belie that teaching. This situation isn't right or wrong, per se. It's just the way it is.

This reason is why, although I have encountered a lot of racism within Christadelphia, I have remained. I don't think it would be **much** better in any other group, and this one at least understands "the Way." Also, I have developed a real affection and love for members of the body.

What I'm getting at is that to combat racism, there needs to be an understanding of our clannish mentality and, more than a willingness, a positive commitment to embracing those without our clans. When Paul writes, "There is neither Jew nor Gentile, neither slave nor free, nor is there male and female, for you are all one in Christ Jesus." (Gal 3:28) he is offering a vision of a body that is one clan.

The uniqueness of our time means we have the wherewithal to obtain this vision on an actual basis rather than an ideal. We can physically interact with those from afar, and we can expand, in fact, our clan and our family. This fact means more than casual interaction and an occasional visit. It means a commitment to entering into relations with those afar. Rather than just telling them they can come to us "any time they want," we need to engage, befriend, mingle with, and live with those not in our group. The onus is NEVER on them; it's always on us.

> If we want to combat racism, we must go live and interact with people who are not like us

If we want to combat racism, we must go live and interact with people who are not like us. This option needs to be meditated upon and considered. Counteracting racism begins with coming to grips with the clannish spirit within us and acting consistently with that understanding.

Peter figured it out. The transition from the Peter of Acts 10:14 (NIV) *"Surely not, Lord!"* Peter replied. *"I have never eaten anything impure or unclean,"* to the Peter of 1 Peter 2:10 (NIV). *"Once you were not a people, but now you are the people of God; once you had not received mercy, but now you have received mercy,"* is a transformation only achievable with the intervention the unstinting assistance of our Savior. It is a journey as far as the east is from the west, and Peter made it.

a Brother

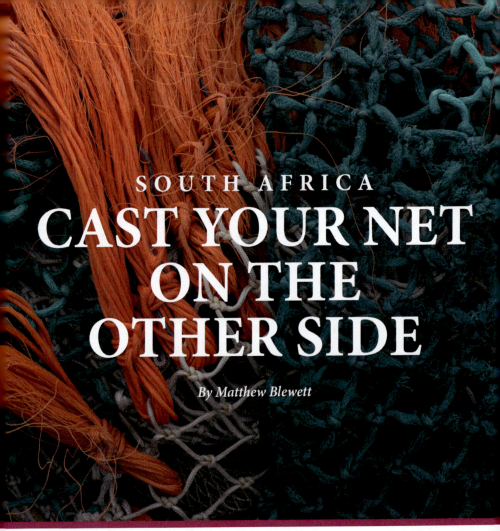

SOUTH AFRICA
CAST YOUR NET ON THE OTHER SIDE

By Matthew Blewett

A CHALLENGE FOR CHANGE

IN July 2005, at the Hebron Haven Bible School in South Africa, a wise and experienced brother issued a challenge for change. A few of us had gathered together to share updates on preaching efforts across the country. The efforts and results, which were much the same as the previous year, could be summarized as sparse. As the meeting drew to a close, the brother spoke for the first time, "If you were in my company, I would fire all of you. Each year, you come back here and report the same poor results using the same methods." After overcoming the shock of his stark assessment, we collectively committed to take up his challenge to change.

At the time, South Africa was experiencing a period of significant transformation, underpinned by a spirit of optimism and new beginnings. Having emerged from a history of segregation under Apartheid over the previous decades, the country was buoyed by a spirit of nationalism and optimism as it prepared to host the world's largest sporting event, the FIFA Soccer World Cup in 2010. The time was ripe for change and progress both in the country and our spiritual community.

Facing Decline

Like in most other countries, preaching efforts in South Africa before 2005 took the form of lectures and seminars presented in existing ecclesial halls, special campaigns at hired venues and correspondence courses sent to students throughout the country. There was little coordination of effort, primarily short-term 12-month planning, and most preaching was concentrated in the wealthier suburbs near established ecclesial halls. Little emphasis was placed on developing long-term relationships with target communities, and welfare was typically limited to members of our own community. Consequently, we scarcely reflected the South African population's diversity, or the transformation experienced throughout the country. To exacerbate the situation, our community was in decline, as many families chose to emigrate to Australia, New Zealand, the United Kingdom and the United States. The 2010

A Campaign is Born

Over the next five years, this context and the challenge to change led to transformation extending beyond our methods of preaching and impacting our community at its core. The **2010 Campaign** was born. Ten years later, its vision, strategy and philosophy continue to ignite our community in South Africa.

The **2010 Campaign** resulted from a unique gathering of many who encouraged long-term planning and out-of-the-box thinking. A strong base of members from various ecclesias in South Africa agreed to support the long-term outreach plan with clear goals, strategies and principles. For all of those present at the time, the ideas and goals posited were way bigger than anything we had ever sought to achieve before. This project required a new level of faith as we faced the prospect of stepping out of our comfort zones into new and untested waters.

Touch and Teach

One of the foundational principles of the **2010 Campaign** was the *"Cast your net on the other side"* philosophy (John 21:6). The first principle of this philosophy was Touch and Teach. In a country where poverty and inequality are amongst the highest in the world, we could no longer manifest the message of our teaching without touching. The more we could integrate these elements of practice and theory, the more we would emulate the method of our Lord in the gospels. In a country characterized by a history of racial mistrust, we soon found that developing a relationship through "touching communities" (direct involvement in real, tangible works) helped turn stony soil into fertile land.

The Good News of the Kingdom of God

Two other themes that emerged early in the **2010 Campaign** have remained cornerstones of preaching in South Africa. The Enablers for Laborers principle challenged us to diversify our preaching methods. Jesus tells us the real constraint in the harvest is not the field of opportunity but rather the lack of workers (Luke 10:2). By creating a diverse range of activities supporting the overall Touch and Teach preaching campaign, the **2010 Campaign** enabled laborers, from teachers to caregivers, from builders to healthcare workers, from musicians to sports enthusiasts. All these roles were combined through coordinated 2010 activities and united under a single preaching theme. We unified our diverse platforms and programs under Jesus' original preaching tagline: the Good News (gospel) of the Kingdom of God (Matt 4:23). From signs at centers (appropriately called Good News Centers) to T-shirts worn by volunteers and decals on motor vehicles, the same message consistently displayed under this divine banner.

The blessings and abundance that followed our stepping out of the boat in 2005 were beyond anything we could have hoped or imagined. The LORD sent laborers, and the field turned white for harvest. After five years, the **2010 Campaign** ended, but the results left us without any doubt the work must continue. **Ignite 2020**, an even more ambitious campaign followed, and this year, we celebrate the conclusion of that program. Over this period, we implemented many innovative platforms and programs. Not all have been effective, but some have endured and remain the central thrust of preaching activities today.

Meeting People Where They Are

Bible Education Centers (BECs) have proven to be a powerful and consistent platform for teaching the Good News in the streets and byways. Today, we operate five BECs located in city centers and urban townships. Not only do the BECs allow us to locate teaching closer to these communities, but they have also provided open and convenient access to Bible teaching. We no longer require the people to come to our suburban ecclesial halls at times convenient for us. The BECs allow us to meet people where they are. A typical BEC stocks a limited number of Bibles in different versions and languages.

The BECs also act as a depot to receive and return lessons from Bible courses and a place to attend live Bible and adult education classes. All BECs host bi-annual graduation celebrations for those who have completed Bible study courses at nearby ecclesial halls to help bridge the gap between Bible education, worship and fellowship. Many current leaders in the **Ignite 2020** campaign first learned the Good News at one of the BECs.

Connecting with Communities

Another key platform has been establishing multi-purpose centers in marginalized communities. These Good News Centers help establish a deep, relevant and consistent relationship with the local community. Over the years, we learned to truly touch people by understanding their needs. Consequently, each Good News Center offers different services and activities tailored to the local community's needs. These include:

- Preschool for children aged two to five
- After-school homework and support classes
- Feeding schemes
- Artisanal training
- Gogos Teas (Gatherings for older women)
- Sports programs

At the heart of every Good News Center is an ecclesia that offers spiritual growth and fellowship. Currently, eight centers are active in communities across the three most populous provinces in South Africa. The Lamontville Good News Center, surrounded by an extremely impoverished informal settlement, was opened on December 7, 2007. Over the past dozen years, it has proved a flagship example of how to build trust and relationships over time. Not only does the center offer a respected preschool and youth development program, but it is also the home to a BEC and thriving ecclesia. Over the years, the center, like many others, has become a key responder to personal and community emergencies. In the darkest days, a hand outstretched is a lifeline for today and a beacon of hope for the future. When such a light shines, it illuminates the path to a future Kingdom where sorrow and sighing will be removed.

Help from Afar

Over the years, the support of local and international volunteers, with their diverse skills, has contributed hugely to the success and growth of the campaign. A partnership with the Prepare-2-Preach (P2P) program, first started in Australia, has resulted in hundreds of young people experiencing and supporting the many platforms and programs. In 2008, the **2010 Campaign** project hosted the Amanzi International Youth Conference, followed by a P2P preaching project, the first of many since hosted at centers across the country. A gathering of over 250 young people from 10 different countries provided a stream of volunteers who returned over the following years. From teachers to musicians, some returned for a few months while others for a few years. Changing lives is life-changing!

Celebrating 2010

In 2010, South Africa hosted the world at the FIFA Soccer World Cup. At the time, our ambitious **2010 Campaign** hosted an international Bible conference. This Bible conference represented the first fruits of the campaign that began five years earlier, evident not just in the number but also in the diversity of the attendees. At this celebration, it became clear the Lord had only started his work in this field. A five-year journey into the unknown now became the foundation to move forward with even greater passion and faith. As brush fires raged on the mountains around the conference venue, a new 10-year campaign was born. **Ignite 2020** continued the many platforms and programs established in the **2010 Campaign**, emphasizing igniting new light stands throughout the country.

Igniting God's Name in the Earth

Ignite 2020 called for a focus on sustainability and the development of local talent to lead and operate the platforms and programs. New ecclesias in urban townships, mostly based at the Good News Centers, provided fertile ground to develop new spiritual leaders who could also actively manage and run the programs. This development led to further nuanced programs such as Breakfast Clubs and the Learn to Earn program. The Breakfast Club provides children with a nutritious breakfast at the center on their way to school. Combined with a short prayer and spiritual lesson, young ones receive natural and spiritual food to extract the best from the day. The Learn to Earn program encourages community members to participate in "learning" activities, which range from attending classes to actively helping the community in cleaning or feeding programs through a reward voucher system.

The vouchers allow the participants to buy items from a thrift shop at the center. In this way, providing for the community's needs is intertwined with a commitment to learning and growth.

We have learned to act in faith and not fear. To be willing to cast our net on the other side. To be willing to try new things. They don't always work, but we learn and grow even then. One of the great lessons of the preaching experiment in South Africa is that we are laborers for the harvest. Any preaching campaign should ultimately have the harvest as its focus. At the outset, our primary focus was, as with many preaching campaigns, about bringing new converts to Christ. But, to borrow from the parable of the Sower, that is just the beginning of a potential harvest. Many seeds will spring up and never produce a harvest. We all grow together through the seasons of life. Creating spaces and opportunities for sowing the seed and growing together has become our focus over the past ten years. We learned how integrated the natural and the spiritual become during this growth process. We have come to understand we don't touch and teach, but rather, we touch to teach and teach to touch! In practical terms, this means our faith manifests the values we share, the hope we aspire to and our complete reliance on the Lord. Through this integration, we move from being missionaries trying to produce a harvest to missionaries becoming a part of that harvest. *"But God gave the increase."* (1 Cor 3:6).

We have learned to act in faith and not fear. To be willing to cast our net on the other side. To be willing to try new things. They don't always work, but we learn and grow even then.

Lessons Abound

As the **Ignite 2020** campaign draws to a close, blessings abound with a fertile opportunity to innovate and grow. We are constantly amazed at how the project has grown. By the numbers, the **Ignite 2020** campaign operates eight Good News Centers and five Bible Education Centers while supporting many associated programs. All of this is made possible by over 30 local full-time volunteers, many part-time volunteers and a steady stream of international volunteers. We have also been incredibly blessed by open-handed donors, especially from the USA. Many of these donors have opened their hands with funding and their hearts and time in coming to South Africa to share in the impact personally.

We have learned we are called to commit to fruitfulness. If we believe our God is abundant, then He will return a good measure pressed down, shaken together and overflowing (Luke 6:38). We have learned to act in faith and not fear. To be willing to cast our net on the other side. To be willing to try new things. We have learned that if we plan for the long term, in humility, knowing the Lord can and will change our plans, we can think and dream bigger. We give ourselves the time and space to tap into the unlimited power of our Lord. We have also learned that we will always leave a place for God in all our planning and organization. We constantly seek His direction and look for signs and guidance from the Lord of the harvest. The past 15 years have passed as if in a moment. We have much we would still love to do. If the Lord remains away, a new campaign will replace **Ignite 2020**. It will carry on the current platforms and programs while reinvigorating us towards innovations and goals.

Looking Forward

As we look forward to an uncertain future, no doubt deeply impacted by the coronavirus crisis, we are sure of a few things. The need for help today and hope tomorrow in our communities will be greater than ever before. The opportunity to provide for such needs has never been better placed. As the world and South Africa pass into this new era, the foundations laid over the past 15 years hold significant potential for eternal impact. May we not retract in fear. May we not grow weary. May we soar on the wings of the eagles that have gone before. May we join Isaiah's timeless refrain, *"Here am I. Send me."* (Isa. 6:8).

Matthew Blewett,
Westville Ecclesia, South Africa

(Reprint of June, 2020 article)

LIFE APPLICATION

ANGER

By Jonathan Farrar

ANGER is an emotion we all experience in ourselves from time to time. Many words are translated as "anger" in the Bible, especially in the Old Testament. The gist is that anger takes on one of two forms: a spontaneous outburst, much like a flame leaping from a match, and a slow burn. Galatians 5 defines inappropriately handled anger as a work of the flesh that will prevent us from inheriting the Kingdom of God. Therefore, it is important to recognize the causes of anger and how to channel this emotion. In this article, we wish to consider how to respond to human anger in ourselves, using the Bible as a guide.

Not all anger is a work of the flesh. For instance, there are many instances of God's anger in the Bible. Still, God is righteous, and His expressions of wrath are always a reaction to a moral wrong, despite individuals' foreknowledge of God's commandments. Similarly, the only recorded incident where Jesus was angry (Mark 3:5) was in connection with a moral wrong—the lack of mercy displayed by the Pharisees, who resented his healing on the Sabbath. In several other instances in Jesus' life, we may infer he was angry. He overturned the money changers' tables for turning the temple courtyard into a retail market and excoriated the Pharisees for their hypocrisy. Jesus did not sin when he was angry, nor did he sin by being angry.

Appropriate vs. Inappropriate Anger
Appropriate anger is a response to a moral wrong and characterizes all the instances of God's and Jesus' anger. On the other hand, inappropriate anger is a reaction to a misperception or a loss of something (such as personal pride) and is always selfish and damaging to others.

Inappropriate Anger
There are many Bible examples of inappropriately angry individuals. Names such as Ahab, Baalam, Asa, Cain, Jonah, Haman, Herod, Naaman, Potiphar, Uzziah, and the prodigal son's older brother may come to mind. A brief synopsis of each follows.

Ahab became vexed and sullen when he did not get his way (1 Kgs 21:4). Baalam misperceived what his donkey was doing and thrice inflicted physical abuse on the hapless animal (Num 22:23-27). Cain's jealous anger towards his brother Abel led to Abel's murder (Gen 4:6-8). Jonah wanted God to exact vengeance on the repentant Ninevites and was inappropriately angry with God when God showed mercy instead (Jonah 3:10; 4:1-3). Haman wanted recognition and admiration following his promotion from Ahasuerus. Still, when Mordecai would not acknowledge Haman's exalted position, Haman became furious (Est 3:5). Instead of being grateful that Elisha had told him how to be healed of his leprosy, Naaman became indignant because Elisha's instructions did not align with his preferences. Had Potiphar made an effort to check with Joseph about the truth of the allegations made by his wife, Potiphar would not have been improperly angry with Joseph. Instead, Potiphar would likely have been acceptably angry at his wife. Asa, Uzziah, and Herod were all rebuked for wrongdoing and became disproportionately angry due to their wounded pride. Rather than be joyful that his brother had returned, the prodigal son seethed with jealous anger that he had never been feted.

These (and other) examples show how easily we can become unduly angry. Furthermore, they show that when individuals respond to their misguided anger, their actions are always sinful and never edify. It is never possible to act in a commendable way when we are unreasonably angry. The antidote is to not become inappropriately angry in the first place.

Avoiding snap judgments, as Jesus taught, *"Judge not according to the appearance."* (John 7:24),[1] and instead getting correct information about a situation is a way to avoid becoming inappropriately angry. To this end, James states, *"My dear brothers and sisters, take note of this: Everyone should be quick to listen, slow to speak, and slow to become angry."* (1:19 NIV). If we are quick to listen, we have tried to get facts from all relevant parties. Otherwise, if we jump to conclusions based on incomplete information, Proverbs sets out the consequences: *"He that answereth a matter before he heareth it, it is folly and shame unto him."* (18:13).

Avoiding regrettable anger caused by wounded pride may be as simple as acknowledging to ourselves and others when we make mistakes. Wanting recognition and not receiving it is a sign of pride. An antidote is to serve others, thereby taking the focus off us. Jealousy is even more potent than anger, regardless of whether anger is a slow burn or a spontaneous outburst. Proverbs states, *"Wrath is cruel, and anger is outrageous; but who is able to stand before envy?"* (27:4). Jealousy is a criticism of God. If God chooses to bless someone and we are jealous of that individual, we are, in effect, telling God that He is wrong to bless someone. Who are we to judge the Almighty's actions? We can avoid jealousy by comparing ourselves only to Christ, thereby learning contentment.

Jesus addresses improper anger when he declares:

> *Ye have heard that it was said of them of old time, Thou shalt not kill; and whoever shall kill shall be in danger of the judgment: But I say unto you, That whosoever is angry with his brother without a cause shall be in danger of the judgment: and whosoever shall say to his brother, Raca, shall be in danger of the council: but whosoever shall say, Thou fool, shall be in danger of hell fire.* (Matt 5:21-22).

Jesus may have been teaching that inappropriate anger is as worthy of punishment as the act of murder. The expression of anger with injurious language is even more worthy of punishment, and acting on

inappropriate anger is even worse than having the feeling. Trying to tame the tongue, with its deadly poison (Jas 3:8), may be next to impossible in this situation. Ideally, we will recognize the status of our anger and immediately take corrective action.

Appropriate Anger

When someone is angry, it is possible to act both inappropriately and appropriately. Moses exemplifies both responses to anger. On two occasions, he acted appropriately, but sandwiched between these occasions was an episode of inappropriate behavior.

In Leviticus, Moses became suitably angry with Aaron, Eleazar, and Ithamar when they disobeyed him and did not eat the sacrificial goat (10:16), an offering Moses had instructed them to eat (10:12-14). The Bible says the priest and his sons were supposed to eat the sin offering (Lev 6:26-29). Moses knew these three individuals had disobeyed his and God's commandment. He also may have been concerned there would be further negative consequences from God, Moses' anger having followed the death of Nadab and Abihu. Aaron responds to Moses by saying,

> Today my sons presented both their sin offering and their burnt offering to the LORD. And yet this tragedy has happened to me [i.e., the death of his other sons Nadab and Abihu]. If I had eaten the people's sin offering on such a tragic day as this, would the LORD have been pleased?" (Lev 10:19 NLT).

Once Moses heard Aaron's response and realized Aaron was grieving and was not intentionally disobedient, he was appeased (10:20).

In Numbers, Moses' appropriate anger is again on display. The Israelites wrongly accused Moses of bringing them into the wilderness to die, as there was no water (20:4), and then heard them complain that the crops in Egypt were nowhere to be found in the wilderness. God told Moses to speak to the rock for the rock to bring forth water. Instead, Moses' frustration with the unreasonable Israelites boiled over, and he smote the rock. Because of his inability to channel his appropriate anger, he was disobedient to God and the resulting punishment was being banned from entering the promised land (20:12). Moses was rightly angered by the false accusations directed at him. However, he acted wrongly. We can all think of more measured, patient ways to deal with that situation, but in the heat of the moment, it is easy to let the flesh take over, just like Moses.

Later in Numbers, Moses was appropriately angry with the warriors of the Israelite army who returned from battle with the Midianites but had not killed the women or children (31:14-16). Although they had not been instructed to kill them, Moses reminded the warriors of the incident in Peor involving sexual immorality with the Moabite women (Numbers 25). Moses seemed to be thinking a repeat performance of sexual immorality could occur, again inviting the (righteous) anger of the LORD (25:3). Moses gave further instructions to the warriors to now kill all the Midianite captives,

It is important to resolve appropriate anger because forgiveness cannot occur until the anger is resolved.

except the young female virgins. And to then undergo a purification process for themselves and the surviving captives. These are the precautions Moses took to prevent a recurrence of the situation in Numbers 25. He viewed the actions of his warriors as inviting sin but then took corrective action.

Other than Moses, there are few Bible examples of individuals who were angry and acted appropriately. Jonathan was aptly angry when his father Saul disgraced him by hurling a spear at him. Still, he did not act amiss, such as insulting his father or hurling the spear back at Saul in retaliation (1 Sam 20:34). Jonathan did get up from the table and leave the room to remove himself from the situation and cool off. Elisha was appropriately angry with King Joash since he only struck the ground three times with arrows (2 Kgs 13:19). Had Joash struck the ground five or six times, he would have wiped out the Syrian army. Elisha did not berate Joash or otherwise act inappropriately because at that time, he was very ill and may have been too weak to do anything other than express frustration reasonably. (2 Kgs 13:14).

Unresolved Appropriate Anger With a Brother or Sister

It is important to resolve appropriate anger because forgiveness cannot occur until the anger is resolved. In his epistle to the Ephesians, Paul sets out a sequence: resolve appropriate anger, and then you will be able to forgive (4:31-32). Have you ever had a time in your life when you were rightly angry with another brother or sister for a moral wrong they committed? Perhaps you followed Jesus' instructions in Matthew 18:15 to talk privately with that person. Perhaps that person refused to talk to you. If you then approached the Arranging Board for assistance (v. 16-17), but they were dismissive, your appropriate anger would not be resolved, despite your efforts to follow the approach set out by Jesus. What is someone to do in this kind of situation?

The example of Jesus may be helpful. During Jesus' trial, he could have been appropriately angry with his captors. His trial was illegal and procedurally unfair many times over. Anyone in Jesus' situation would have been naturally angry. Except Jesus. What was his response? *"Father, forgive them; for they know not what they do."* (Luke 23:34). How could Jesus forgive his captors? The answer is, he must have put away his anger before he could forgive. Paul outlined this sequence in Ephesians 4:31-32: Put away anger before forgiveness can occur. I suggest that when Jesus said, *"for they know not what they do,"* he was resolving any inappropriate anger he may have felt. A paraphrase of Jesus' words in Luke 23:34 may be, "Father, forgive them; for they are making mistakes."

If we are ever appropriately angry with someone, it is because they have made a mistake. Acknowledging that others make mistakes, as Jesus acknowledged, is an antidote to appropriate anger. We can relate to mistakes in others because we have all made mistakes. Jesus did not sin, yet could still relate to missteps in others.

To address the question of unresolved appropriate anger, Peter also directs us to the example of Jesus: *"Who, when he was reviled, reviled not again; when he suffered, he threatened not; but committed himself to him that judgeth righteously."* (1 Pet 2:23). What did Jesus do? He committed himself to God to judge righteously. He turned his situation over to God. That may be what we must do. God is the righteous judge. If the wisdom or justice of God dictates that punishment is deserved, God will do that according to His timing. Vengeance belongs to God, not to us.

In the context of human anger, Paul commanded the Ephesian brethren not to sin when angry (Eph 4:26). This commandment is sensible if it refers to appropriate anger regarding another's moral wrong. Dealing with proper anger is a difficult test of one's character. To acknowledge someone is making a mistake will go a long way toward resolving the anger. Suppose we cannot converse with someone about their mistake or effect resolution in an ecclesial situation. In that case, we will have to turn the situation over to God in prayer and trust He will judge the situation on His terms.

Conclusion

Love attracts, and anger repels. No one wants to feel angry, and no one wants to be in the company of an angry person. Learning to avoid inappropriate anger is challenging. Learning to channel appropriate anger is also challenging. The Bible supplies many examples of both types of anger.

The example of Jesus should inspire us. He resolved any anger he may have felt at his trial by acknowledging his detractors had made mistakes. Turning his situation over to God to judge righteously, settled the situation for him. It should also do the same for us.

Jonathan Farrar,
Mountain Grove Ecclesia, ON

---

1. All Scriptural citations are taken from the New King James Version unless otherwise noted.

SPECIAL SECTION: **PRAYER**

THE APOSTLE PAUL: PRAYING ON BEHALF OF OTHERS

By Shawn Moynihan

When one reads the Apostle Paul's letters, one is struck by how often he prays for others. He is devoted to praying on others' behalf. Paul is also firmly convinced that he needs others to pray for him. At least eight times, Paul asks others to pray for him (Rom 15:30-32; 2 Cor 1:10-11; Eph 6:18-20; Phil 1:19; Col 4:2-4; 1 Thess 5:25; 2 Thess 3:1-2; Phm 1:22). Paul's teaching about prayer is based on the fundamental principle that praying for others is important and purposeful, for both the one praying and the one being prayed for:

> First of all, then, I urge that supplications, prayers, intercessions, and thanksgivings be made for all people, for kings and all who are in high positions, that we may lead a peaceful and quiet life, godly and dignified in every way. This is good, and it is pleasing in the sight of God our Savior, who desires all people to be saved and to come to the knowledge of the truth. (1 Tim 2:1-4 ESV).

To pray on behalf of others is to do a good thing that pleases God, impacting both the one praying and the one being prayed for.

Paul's exhortation to Timothy packs a lot of teaching into a few sentences. Praying for others is foundational. "First" is the Greek *proton*, denoting temporal, or conceptual primacy. We are to pray for all people, even people who are clearly not in the household of faith (e.g., the many secular rulers with whom Paul and the early ecclesia interacted). Our prayers for others are built on the premise that our will is aligned with God's in an important way; namely, we have the shared desire for others to come to the knowledge of gospel truth, to repent, to be baptized, and to be saved through God's grace. Bro. Cyril Tennant comments on this important facet, stating that there is a "much deeper significance to praying for others—it is a reflection of our own understanding regarding salvation."[1] In praying for others, we acknowledge God's mercy towards us and ask that others' have the same blessing:

> The Lord is not slack concerning His promise, as some count slackness, but is longsuffering toward us, not willing that any should perish but that all should come to repentance. (2 Pet 3:9).[2]

Prayer Actions

In his exhortation to Timothy, Paul lists specific prayer actions that we must engage in on behalf of others: supplications (*deésis*), prayers (*proseuché*), intercessions (*enteuxis*), and giving of thanks (*eucharistia*). Although *deésis* can refer to the general practice of prayer (e.g., 2 Tim 1:3), it seems to be used often in the context of asking for something specific. For example, Paul states that the supplications of others helped keep him safe (2 Cor 1:9-11; Phil 1:19) and in Ephesians 6:18-20, Paul uses the word to refer to requests that he preach the gospel boldly. James also uses the word to describe a specific request to God on others' behalf:

Confess your trespasses to one another, and pray for one another, that you may be healed. The effective, fervent prayer [deésis] of a righteous man avails much. (Jas 5:16).

As James asserts, in some cases where the need is not evident, our specific requests to God for others requires a relationship of mutual trust so that the need is made manifest. As I reflect on making supplication for others, I am moved to ask, "Do I know my brothers and sisters well enough to make supplication for them?" James is not only teaching about the power of prayer on behalf of others; he is teaching about the power of prayer that is founded on honest and genuine relationships between believers.

Intercession

The word translated *"intercessions"* in 1 Timothy 2 is a rare one, used only one other time: *"For every creature of God is good, and nothing is to be refused if it is received with thanksgiving; for it is sanctified by the word of God and prayer [enteuxis]."* (1 Tim 4:4-5). In the context of prayer, the verb form of the word (*entugchanó*) is used to describe Elijah's prayers to God against Israel (Rom 11:2) and to describe Christ's current work (Rom 8:27, 34; Heb 7:25).

In praying on behalf of others, we acknowledge that our prayers of intercession pale in comparison to Christ's work on our behalf. Paul acknowledges this in the context of his teaching regarding praying for others:

Therefore I exhort first of all that supplications, prayers, intercessions, and giving of thanks be made for all men...For there is one God and one Mediator between God and men, the Man Christ Jesus. (1 Tim 2:1-5).

Clause 14 of the BASF states that Jesus:

Is a priest over his own house only, and does not intercede for the world, or for professors who are abandoned to disobedience...he makes intercession for his erring brethren, if they confess and forsake their sins (Luke 24:51; Ephesians 1:20; Acts 5:31; 1 Timothy 2:5; Hebrews 8:1; Acts 15:14; 13:39; Hebrews 4:14, 15; John 17:9; Hebrews 10:26; 1 John 2:1; Proverbs 28:13).

Unlike us, Christ has the power of God, and unlike us, his will is completely aligned with God's (Rom 8:27). Unlike us, he has a unique place of power from which to intercede (Rom 8:34). Unlike us, Christ's intercession is continual (Heb 7:25).

Given that we can add nothing to the effectiveness of Jesus' intercession, why does Paul exhort us that intercessions be made on others' behalf? Paul was acutely aware of Christ's efficacy as an intercessor, yet he repeatedly asked for others to pray for him. James tells us that our prayers for others are impactful: *"The active prayer of a righteous person has great power."* (James 5:16 Mounce).

Paul knew that praying for others makes us focus on their needs, not ours, helping to develop a Christ-like mind in us. Individually and collectively, we are strengthened by praying for each other. Bro. Alfred Nicholls wrote,

> The important thing is… that the intercession should be made, if not in public then by each of us in private… The ministry of prayer is something in which all can engage and many can testify to the strength, courage and increased faith that comes from the knowledge that others, individually or collectively, remember them 'without ceasing' in their prayers.[3]

Peter seems to have this in mind in 1 Peter 3, where he quotes Psalm 34 (*"His ears are open to their prayers"*) to describe prayer as a tangible action stemming from the exhortation to *"be like-minded, be sympathetic, love one another, be compassionate and humble."* (v. 8 NIV).

Giving Thanks for Others

When it comes to praying on behalf of our brothers and sisters in Christ, where do we start? Paul's starting point was to be thankful for his family in Christ. For Paul, giving thanks in this way was something that he "owed" (Greek *opheilō*):

> We are bound [*opheilō*] to thank God always for you, brethren. (2 Thess 1: 3).

> But we are bound [*opheilō*] to give thanks to God always for you, brethren beloved by the Lord, because God from the beginning chose you for salvation through sanctification by the Spirit and belief in the truth, to which He called you by our gospel, for the obtaining of the glory of our Lord Jesus Christ. (2 Thess 2:13-14).

Paul recognized that we were indebted to each other because we needed each other. Every member of the Body is valued and valuable. We are blessed to have brothers and sisters who can help build up our faith and we give thanks to God for this blessing.

Paul was thankful for the experiences that he shared with brothers and sisters. To the ecclesia at Philippi, Paul wrote:

> *I thank my God upon every remembrance of you, always in every prayer of mine making request for you all with joy, for your fellowship in the gospel from the first day until now."* (Phil 1:3-5).

Similarly, Paul told the ecclesia at Thessalonica:

> We give thanks to God always for you all, making mention of you in our prayers, remembering without ceasing your work of faith, labor of love, and patience of hope in our Lord Jesus Christ in the sight of our God and Father, knowing, beloved brethren, your election by God. (1 Thess 1:2-4).

This kind of thanksgiving prayer is easy to give for those I know well, because it is grounded in common experiences and shaped by shared memories.

The closer the relationship, the easier it is to be thankful for the other members of One Body. Paul's close relationship with Timothy was expressed in prayers of thanksgiving:

> I thank God, whom I serve with a pure conscience, as my forefathers did, as without ceasing I remember you in my prayers night and day, greatly desiring to see you, being mindful of your tears, that I may be filled with joy, when I call to remembrance the genuine faith that is in you, which dwelt first in your grandmother Lois and your mother Eunice, and I am persuaded is in you also. (2 Tim 1:3-5).

One of the great blessings of a life as a part of the One Body is a collection of deep and rich personal relationships, some new and some of which span decades and generations. Like Paul, I give thanks to God for my brothers and sisters, as well as their parents and grandparents. I also give thanks that I know them, their tears, their joys, their struggles, their victories, and their needs.

Always and Without Ceasing

If being thankful was the first thing that Paul thought of when he was praying for others, then it seems that it was also the second, third, and fourth thing. Paul asserts in several places that he is *"always," "without ceasing,"* offering prayers of thanksgiving to God for other members of the Body:

> First, I thank my God through Jesus Christ for you all… **without ceasing** I make mention of you always in my prayers." (Rom 1: 8-9).

> I thank my God **always** concerning you for the grace of God which was given to you by Christ Jesus. (1 Cor 1:4).

> Therefore I also, after I heard of your faith in the Lord Jesus and your love for all the saints, **do not cease** to give thanks for you, making mention of you in my prayers. (Eph 1:15-16).

> We give thanks to the God and Father of our Lord Jesus Christ, praying **always** for you, since we heard of your faith in Christ Jesus and of your love for all the saints. (Col 1: 3-4).

> I thank my God, making mention of you **always** in my prayers. (Phm 1: 4).

Paul exhorts us to *"always keep on praying for all the Lord's people."* (Eph 6:19 NIV). By his words and his actions, Paul is teaching us that praying for each other begins with thanksgiving.

Thanksgiving Changes the Way We View Each Other

How would our ecclesias be different if we made thanksgiving for each other the consistent starting point when we prayed for our brothers and sisters in Christ? How would the worldwide Body be different? I have tried this in my own prayer life, and it changed me, especially in contentious matters. My prayers on behalf of others used to focus on differences. Frequently my prayers devolved into a variation of me asking God to help other members of the Body see things my way. Building on the metaphor of the One Body in 1 Corinthians 12:12-27, I was essentially asking God to make the "hand" be like the "eye." When my prayers changed

How would our ecclesias be different if we made thanksgiving for each other the consistent starting point when we prayed for our brothers and sisters in Christ?

to simply being thankful to God for the members of the Body, who were different from me, and trusting God's wisdom in arranging the Body in keeping with His purpose, then my attitude towards my brothers was positively transformed. It made me understand, and be thankful for the truth of Paul's statement: *"God arranged the members in the body, each one of them, as he chose."* (1 Cor 12:18 ESV).

Again, Paul's example is powerful. In 1 Timothy 2:1-4, Paul is teaching us to pray for others who are actively seeking our harm. His teaching regarding prayers on behalf of *"kings and all who are in high positions"* had special resonance for Paul. He likely wrote 1 Timothy following his first imprisonment at Rome; therefore, he was praying for the very people who had jailed him and who would ultimately sentence him to death. Paul takes this same prayerful approach to Jewish rulers who persistently sought to kill him: *"Brethren, my heart's desire and prayer to God for Israel is that they may be saved."* (Rom 10:1). Both the Jewish and Gentile authorities caused Paul great harm and anguish; however, he prayed that they might be saved. In praying for his enemies, Paul recognized that he was once the beneficiary of Stephen's prayer for him to be forgiven. (Acts 7:57-60).

In 2 Thessalonians 2:13-14, Paul states that he is *"bound"* to always give thanks for the members at Thessalonica *"because God from the beginning chose you for salvation."* Paul recognized that he didn't choose the members of the One Body—God did. Therefore, Paul gave thanks for those at Thessalonica, even though these were the some of the very same people who earlier leveled a series of slanderous accusations (see Paul's response in 1 Thessalonians 2).[4] I have found it very challenging to pray on behalf of those other members of the Body who, through words and actions, expressed "I have no need of you." Yet Paul shows me how to enact Jesus' admonition to *"pray for anyone who mistreats you."* (Matt 5:44 CEV). In seeking a restored relationship, a crucial step is praying for those with whom there is conflict: *"So the Lord restored what Job had lost after he prayed for his friends."* (Job 42:10 NET).

Prayer as a Joint Struggle

Paul teaches us that if we pray for others, then we are joining them in their struggle. Paul tells the ecclesia at Rome:

> Brothers and sisters, I urge you, through our Lord Jesus Christ and through the love of the Spirit, **to join me in my struggles** in your prayers to God for me. (Rom 15:30 CEB).

Paul commends Epaphras for this:

> Epaphras, who is one of you, a servant of Christ Jesus, greets you, **always struggling on your behalf in his prayers**, that you may stand mature and fully assured in all the will of God. (Col 4:12 ESV).

The Greek word *agon*, which had powerful semantic associations in the Greco-Roman world (i.e., a public contest, such as an athletic event, where the struggle was both noble and beautiful), is the root for these descriptions of prayer on others' behalf.

A cognate of this Greek word also describes Jesus praying through his most demanding struggle, *"And being in agony [agónia], He prayed more earnestly."* (Luke 22:44). It is interesting to note that Jesus asked Peter, James, and John to *"watch and pray"* about their temptation while he too was praying. Rather than supporting Jesus, the three fell asleep and an angel was sent to strengthen Jesus (Luke 22:43). Sometimes, it is easy to grow weary and not support others. It is easy to feel like we are mere spectators in the struggles faced by our brothers and sisters. It is similarly easy to feel that we are alone in our own struggles. However, Paul teaches us that we are not spectators. By praying for others who struggle, we are in the fight with them. Neither are we alone in the arena when our brothers and sisters pray on our behalf.

When We Pray for Others, What Do We Say?

In some cases, it is clear what to pray for. Deliverance from illness, injury, and dangerous circumstances are axiomatic things for which to pray. Paul invites others to pray for him in these circumstances. He asks the ecclesia at Rome to pray for his deliverance from the Judaizers in Jerusalem (Rom 15:31). Paul states that the prayers of the Corinthian brothers and sisters aided his deliverance from death: *"who delivered us from so great a death, and does deliver us; in whom we trust that He will still deliver us, you also helping together in prayer for us."* (2 Cor 1:10-11). Paul commends the Philippian ecclesia for their prayers on his behalf, addressing the circumstances of his imprisonment: *"For I know that this will turn out for my deliverance through your prayer."* (Phil 1:19). Similarly, Paul invites the believers at Thessalonica to pray for his deliverance: *"Finally, brethren, pray for us… that we may be delivered from unreasonable and wicked men."* (2 Thess 3:1-2).

As it was for Paul in the first century, so it is for us in the twenty-first century. We know what to pray for when brothers and sisters are physically sick or injured. We know what to pray for when they are persecuted and in danger. We know what to pray for when there are tragedies and natural disasters. We know what to pray for when others' challenges are visible.

However, many challenges are not visible. Spiritual, mental, and emotional struggles are not always apparent. Relationship challenges are not always observable. Even areas of apparent strength can be real challenges for us. Paul humbly revealed some of his challenges and asked others to pray for him.

We think of Paul as a gifted and fearless proclaimer of the gospel. However, this is the very thing that he asked his brothers and sisters in Ephesus to pray for:

> *Pray also for me, that whenever I speak, words may be given me so* **that I will fearlessly make known the mystery of the gospel,** *for which I am an ambassador in chains. Pray that I may* **declare it fearlessly,** *as I should.* (Eph 6:19-20 NIV).

Similarly, he implored the believers in Colossae:

> And pray for us, too, that God may open a door for our message, so that we may proclaim the mystery of Christ, for which I am in chains. Pray *that I may proclaim it clearly*, as I should. (Col 4:3-4 NIV).

Paul trusted his relationships with other members of Christ's Body; therefore, he disclosed some of the challenges he was facing and asked others to pray for him.

Paul's critics highlight the very things that he humbly asked others to pray for on his behalf. In 2 Corinthians 10:10, he quotes his critics: *"'For his letters,' they say, 'are weighty and powerful, but his bodily presence is weak, and his speech contemptible.'"* Paul is accused of being timid in person, but he asks for prayers to fearlessly declare his message. He is accused of being a poor oral communicator, yet Paul asks for prayers that he be clear in his communication of the gospel. This is a powerful lesson for all of us. Perhaps the best way to respond when others criticize us (fairly or unfairly) is to ask for their help through prayer.

Being Bold on Behalf of Others

Perhaps the best summary of Paul's prayers on behalf of others is found in Ephesians, where his two longest prayers are recorded (Eph 1:16-21; Eph 3:14-21). Boldness in prayer was on Paul's mind. His digression that interrupts his prayer in chapter 3 is punctuated by *"Christ Jesus our Lord, in whom we have boldness and access with confidence through faith in Him."* (v. 11-12).

In the first chapter, Paul asks that God help believers to fully appreciate the greatness of His plans for them and the *"exceeding greatness of His power toward us who believe, according to the working of His mighty power."* (Eph 1:19). Essentially, Paul prays that the believers at Ephesus can understand something that strains the limit of human comprehension. Paul asks that:

> The God of our Lord Jesus Christ, the Father of glory, may give to you the spirit of wisdom and revelation in the knowledge of Him, the eyes of your understanding being enlightened; that you may know what is the hope of His calling, what are the riches of the glory of His inheritance in the saints, and what is the exceeding greatness of His power toward us who believe, according to the working of His mighty power. (Eph 1:17-19).

God's blessings to us are so profound that we can only understand them when He enables *"the eyes of... understanding being enlightened."*

Paul's prayer in Ephesians 3 is similarly bold. Here, Paul uses the concept of the family (*patria*) following the Father's (*pater*) example to contextualize his prayer. On behalf of the Ephesians, he petitions the Father to:

- Strengthen with might through His Spirit in the inner man.
- Have Christ dwell in hearts through faith.
- Root and ground in love.
- Enable collective comprehension of the four dimensions of Christ's love.
- Fill with His fullness.

Paul asks that God help the believers at Ephesus move beyond simple intellectual knowledge of God and Jesus. Paul asks that the believers' characters be like God and Jesus. Bro. John Carter explains the intent of Paul's prayer in this way:

> The very climax of the prayer is that the saints may be filled with the fullness of God. It is a bold and amazing thing that is here desired. The words, few and simple, easily slipped over in the reading of the chapter, express the highest possible aim of mortal man. All that God is, they must try to be. The Son of God was manifested to make it possible... When a man receives of the grace and truth that came by Jesus, and of which he was "full," he is justified. But he must go on to perfection.[5]

Paul's example shows us that we can "go big" when praying for others. We can pray that others manifest God's character, that the members of God's family demonstrate the attributes of the Father.

Final Words

Paul prayed that others might be saved. That was his purpose in his near constant prayers on others' behalf and in his frequent requests that others pray for him. We, too, pray that God will save the other members of the One Body and ask for their prayers. Our prayers for others are purposeful, effective, and transformative, especially when use thanksgiving as the starting point. We will give Paul the final word:

> *Now may the God of peace Himself sanctify you completely; and may your whole spirit, soul, and body be preserved blameless at the coming of our Lord Jesus Christ. He who calls you is faithful, who also will do it. Brethren, pray for us.* (1 Thess 5:23-25).

Shawn Moynihan,
Cambridge Ecclesia, ON

---

1. Tennant, Cyril, *The Prayers of Paul*, The Christadelphian, Jan 2007.
2. All Scriptural citations are taken from the New King James Version, unless specifically noted.
3. Nicholls, Alfred, *The Christadelphian*, April 1979.
4. William Barclay notes that "Beneath the surface of this passage run the slanders which Paul's opponents at Thessalonica attached to him." (*William Barclay's Daily Study Bible*: 1 Thessalonians).
5. Carter, John, *The Letter to the Ephesians*, The Christadelphian Publishing Association, 1944.

EXHORTATION AND CONSOLATION

TECHNOLOGY AND THE ECCLESIA

By Jonathan Schwieger, Jr.

TODAY I stand before you to shed light on a topic that has become an integral part of our lives: technology. In this rapidly advancing world, where innovation is transforming the way we live, work, and communicate, it is crucial for us, as Christadelphians, to understand and appreciate the benefits that technology brings. While there are potential pitfalls, let us explore how we can harness technology to enhance our spiritual journey and spread the light of God's Word.

One of the remarkable advantages of technology is its ability to connect people across vast distances. In our interconnected world, we can communicate with brothers and sisters in Christadelphian communities worldwide, instantly sharing our experiences, prayers, and encouragement. Through video calls, online forums, and social media platforms, we can extend the reach of our fellowship, fostering a sense of unity and support beyond physical boundaries.

Let us not forget the power of technology in disseminating the gospel. With the advent of the Internet, we have witnessed an unprecedented opportunity to reach out to a global audience with the Word of God. Websites, podcasts, and online publications enable us to share Bible studies, sermons, and teachings, ensuring that the message of salvation can reach corners of the world previously untouched by our physical presence.

Technology has provided us with a wealth of knowledge at our fingertips. Through online libraries, educational resources, and digital study tools, we can deepen our understanding of Scripture and explore biblical truths with greater efficiency. The availability of commentaries, concordances, and translations allows us to delve into the Word of God, strengthening our faith and equipping us for the challenges we face.

Additionally, advancements in technology have granted us access to historical and archaeological discoveries, enriching our comprehension of biblical events and contexts. We can explore virtual tours of ancient sites, examine digitized manuscripts, and engage in scholarly discussions, enhancing our appreciation for the Scriptures and enabling us to defend our beliefs with confidence.

While we must be cautious not to let technology dominate our lives, we can leverage it to better steward the resources entrusted to us. Energy-efficient technologies, sustainable practices, and environmentally conscious solutions align with our responsibility to care for God's creation. By utilizing technology wisely, we can reduce waste, conserve resources, and strive for a more sustainable future.

Moreover, technology has revolutionized the way we manage time and resources. From digital calendars and productivity tools to online collaboration platforms, we can optimize our efforts and dedicate more time to serving others and advancing God's Kingdom. By embracing technology's efficiency, we can free ourselves from menial tasks and focus on fulfilling our purpose as ambassadors of Christ.

Let us remember that technology, like any tool, is neither inherently good nor evil. Its value lies in how we choose to utilize it. May we approach technology with wisdom, guided by the Holy Spirit, as we strive to bring glory to God and shine His light in a world that increasingly relies on technology. Amen.

However, we must not overlook the potential dangers and pitfalls tech presents. As followers of Christ, we are called to be discerning and wise in our choices, mindful of the spiritual and moral implications of the technologies we embrace.

In this fast-paced world, technology offers us the allure of instant gratification. The Internet grants us access to a wealth of information at our fingertips, entertainment at any moment, and a multitude of social connections. However, we must guard against the subtle dangers that lie within this instant gratification. Our time spent online can easily distract us from our spiritual priorities, leading to a neglect of prayer, Bible study, and fellowship. Let us remember that true fulfillment lies in communion with God and our brothers and sisters, not solely in the fleeting pleasures offered by technology.

While technology enables us to connect with others across vast distances, it also threatens to erode genuine relationships. Social media, for instance, can create an illusion of connectedness while fostering superficiality and comparison. We may find ourselves engrossed in endless scrolling, seeking validation through likes and comments, rather than cultivating authentic bonds with our loved ones. As Christadelphians, we are called to love one another deeply, to bear one another's burdens, and to build genuine connections. Let us be mindful of the ways in which technology can hinder this mission and take deliberate steps to foster real, meaningful relationships.

Advancements in technology often outpace the moral compass of society. In this digital age, we are bombarded with content that can be morally compromising and even destructive to our souls. Pornography, violence, and materialistic ideologies are easily accessible, posing significant challenges to our spiritual well-being. As followers of Christ, we must actively guard our hearts and minds, filtering our media consumption and embracing discernment. Let us hold fast to the words of Philippians 4:8 (NIV), *"Finally, brothers and sisters, whatever is true, whatever is noble, whatever is right, whatever is pure, whatever is lovely, whatever is admirable—if anything is excellent or praiseworthy—think about such things."*

Technology, when misused, can become an idol in our lives. The pursuit of the latest gadgets, the constant need for virtual validation, and the obsession with digital fame can lead us away from our true purpose—glorifying God. Let us not allow our possessions or online personas to take precedence over our relationship with our Heavenly Father. Instead, may we use technology as a tool for His glory, to spread His message, and to serve others in love.

Conclusion:

As Christadelphians, we are called to engage with the world while remaining grounded in our faith. Technology, when embraced with discernment, can be a powerful tool for fulfilling our mission. Through communication and connectivity, we can strengthen our global fellowship, spreading love and support to brothers and sisters worldwide. By accessing knowledge and understanding, we can deepen our understanding of God's Word and share its life-transforming message more effectively. Finally, by embracing stewardship and efficiency, we can optimize our resources and dedicate ourselves more fully to God's work. And let us remember that technology itself is not inherently evil, but rather it is the way in which we engage with it that can lead to peril. By approaching technology with wisdom, discernment, and a Christ-centered perspective, we can harness its potential for good while safeguarding ourselves from its perils. May we prioritize our spiritual growth, foster genuine relationships, and remain steadfast in our commitment to Christ. Let us pray for God's guidance and strength in navigating the digital age with wisdom, so that we may shine as lights in the world, reflecting the love and truth of our Savior, Jesus Christ.

The Real Exhortation

Now, the exhortation I just gave on technology may be a first for Christadelphians. Not because the topic is on technology, which I am sure others have delved into, but a first because it was written entirely by Artificial Intelligence (AI). That's right, I didn't write a word of it until this point. I used ChatGPT and asked it to do the following: first, "From a Christadelphian perspective, write an exhortation on the benefits of technology" and then, "From a Christadelphian perspective, write an exhortation on the perils of technology." I then merged those two into today's exhortation. I intended to see if the ultimate technological advancement in today's age would be capable of using algorithms to accurately express what I think about the use of technology, at the same time, including a slant from our beliefs. I did notice a lack of Bible quotations to support the comments. There was excessive use of the passive voice. And some words were not part of my usual vocabulary. But, overall, it was pretty spot-on when it comes to outlining the advantages and disadvantages of tech and how we use it to:

- Increase our knowledge of God's Word, as we see in Romans 15:4 (NKJV) *"For whatever was written in former days was written for our instruction, that through endurance and through the encouragement of the Scriptures we might have hope."*

- Spread the knowledge of God's Word, as commanded in Mark 16:15 (ESV), *"Go into all the world and proclaim the gospel to the whole creation."*

- Uncover the pitfalls of misinformation and disinformation that can come from technology. We read in 2 Peter 2:1 (ESV), *"But false prophets also arose among the people, just as there will be false teachers among you, who will secretly bring in destructive heresies, even denying the Master who bought them, bringing upon themselves swift destruction."*

- Be responsible for ensuring what AI writes is correct. If used alone for exhortations and Bible classes, it may lead to the laziness of scholarship. We still need to study the passages and look for insights and wisdom. It should never replace (only supplement) our personal study. *"These were more fair-minded than those in Thessalonica, in that they received the word with all readiness, and searched the Scriptures daily to find out whether these things were so."* (Acts 17:11 NKJV).

We all have heard about lots of technology phobias, going back to radio and TV. Each time, we have found a way to use the new technology for good to promote the gospel. The Internet, for example, was touted as a terrible new technology that would destroy our young people. Some of that may be true, but we have been able to use it to proclaim the gospel in unprecedented ways around the entire world. So, the premise is certainly correct; we need to harness it for good.

Whichever way you fall on the overall use of tech, whether it's computers, tablets, phones, Internet or AI, I believe that (as with most things) it's all about moderation and intent, as our ChatGPT overlords have pointed out. But this concept goes far beyond just the use of technology; it can also be a part of anything in our lives. 1 Corinthians 9:25: *"And everyone who competes for the prize is temperate in all things."*

I sometimes wonder how people of the Bible age would view us and the various technological advances at our fingertips. Would they be appalled at how tech has caused us to drift away from the Word of God and the message of Jesus Christ? Or would they be impressed at how quickly we can disseminate the Word to people worldwide and spread the Good News of the sacrifice of our Lord Jesus Christ? I do know they would want us here, at the Memorial Table, each week, remembering our Lord in the same manner they did.

*Jonathan Schwieger, Jr.,
Pittsburgh Ecclesia, PA*

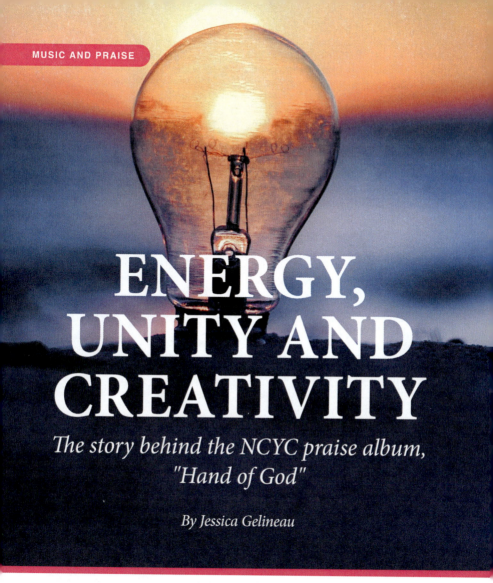

MUSIC AND PRAISE

ENERGY, UNITY AND CREATIVITY

The story behind the NCYC praise album, "Hand of God"

By Jessica Gelineau

ON June 6th, 2023, Bro. Levi Myers (Cambridge, ON) and Bro. Levi Gelineau (Simi Hills, CA) spoke with Sis. Hayley Dangerfield (Gosford, NSW, Australia) and Bro. Gideon Ryan (Hunter Valley, NSW, Australia) about their youth group's energetic musical project, creating a brand-new album titled "Hand of God." The four discuss the initial project goal of reenergizing the CYC post-lockdown and the continuing impact this unique project has had in unifying young people and whole ecclesias through teamwork, cooperation, and praise. The full version of this conversation is featured in Episode 9 of the Good Christadelphian Music podcast, available on whatever platform you use for podcast listening!

Levi M: You've all done a great job on this project. Give us some background on how it came into being.

Hayley D: The idea came about at the end of 2020. As we all know, the world was in lockdown for a lot of that year, so that definitely impacted our youth group. Gideon and I are from Newcastle CYC (NCYC), and around sixty to eighty young people attend. It was tricky for the youth group to be in lockdown—not being able to socialize and having everything on Zoom. Being on the committee for that youth group, I was brainstorming a few ideas of what we could do over the next year once the lockdown lifted to reignite the passion in our youth group and bring everyone back together. The Brisbane CYC had done an album, "Stand Firm," which came out at the end of 2020. We thought that was a really good album, and if they could do it, we could do it. So we pitched the idea to the committee, and the committee was on board! We then formed a subcommittee and got the idea going. It was a bit of an easy decision to go with music, as our youth group has always had a talent in that area. We've always been passionate about our music and our songs. None of us had composed much before, but it made so much sense to use the talent in our area and go down the music track.

Levi M: That's great. And Gideon, what was your involvement in all that?

Gideon R: I was young when the idea started, still in high school. I joined in on the project straight away cause I thought it was an awesome idea. At first, I didn't have much involvement apart from making a song for the album "Man of Dust." But then, once it

Scenes from the recording weekends at Heritage College Lake Macquarie. Musicians and techs were supported by the nearby ecclesias in many generous ways. Food was brought in for those who were working on the recordings, from dawn until dusk!

got to recording, which didn't happen for a while, I was the guy in the chair for the couple of weekends that we did it, at Heritage College Lake Macquarie. Then I worked on a bunch of post-production as well, with Bro. Joe Cheek, who was our producer on it.

Levi G: There are ten tracks. How many different writers are there?

Hayley D: Every song is a different composer, and some of the songs have multiple composers. Our youngest composer was 14, and our oldest composer was 26. There was a good range of ages.

Levi G: That makes sense then that the styles are a little different through the songs, which also makes it enjoyable by the way to listen to them. It's not the same thing over and over. It's amazing there are over ten different writers for the ten tracks!

Hayley D: We wanted to emphasize distinctive styles. We wanted a range of congregational music and also some meditational pieces. We wanted to encourage lots of different instruments as well. For most composers, it was the first spiritual song they had ever written. So we wanted to drop the expectations and say, "We're not aiming for perfection. Just give it a go." It ended up working out well because it meant we had a great variety of styles and many different people contributing.

Levi M: It's such a wide range of different sounds and styles that it became a complex album. I think that's kind of the beauty of it; trying to be easy and simple with it, you turned it into something unique. The range of voices also adds to the beauty of the resulting product.

Gideon R: We also didn't give anyone a theme to go on. So, the prompt was just to make a praise song you are passionate about. We didn't produce a theme or the title of it until all the songs were recorded. "Hand of God" is a vague, broad term that could apply to anything. Still, it just meant that people sought out the opportunity and made something they were super passionate about, and I think that worked well and didn't constrict anyone.

Levi G: How much communication was happening during the writing process? Or was it more like ten people went away, and ten people came back with finished songs?

Hayley D: We had a night where we got everyone to come together and brainstorm ideas. Then we just said, it's up to you if you want to compose a song. We'll leave it in your hands. Go away, write it, and then let us know, and you can play it live on one of our NCYC activity nights. So we had one of the songs played at our bonfire night. One of the songs played on our praise night, for example. Then, if we liked it and wanted it recorded, they submitted it to be reviewed for recording.

Levi G: Who was reviewing it?

Hayley D: We had some older, more experienced musicians and composers in our area get together one night, and they listened to all the songs. And they also reviewed the lyrics, just making sure that the song was Scriptural, and sent back some feedback on what needed editing. We also had a night

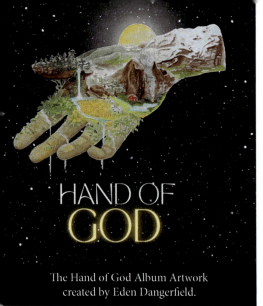

The Hand of God Album Artwork created by Eden Dangerfield.

where those older, more experienced musicians met up with the composers and actually gave them feedback in person as well.

Levi G: And then when did Bro. Joe Cheek get involved? Sorry, I'm getting so technical. I just think it's fascinating!

Hayley D: That was in February or March 2023. So we didn't give him a lot of time! The Adelaide Youth Conference was coming up and we wanted our album to be released when a lot of people could hear it all at once and there would be good hype around it. He smashed the songs out in time for the conference, which was awesome. We have an Australasian Youth Conference every two years, and it changes cities in Australia. So it was pretty big. About 450 young people were there from all around Australia and the entire world! We got to announce it on the conference's final day and then released all the songs on the album that same day. A lot of people were stoked about it.

Levi M: I saw some of the videos on Instagram of the Youth Conference singing the song "Armour of Light," which sounded so good. What better way to launch an album than to have that many young people singing a song all together, all hyped from Bible School. Then that's like your track to go download for the drive home!

Hayley D: Yes, that was exciting, releasing "Armour of Light" at the Conference. We sang it there as a meditation, and then later on, we sang it in the congregation, and everyone picked it up straight away. Sis. Annie Ryan, the composer of that song, even surprised everyone with an acapella part; everyone still sang it right, and it sounded amazing. It was an easy one to pick up.

Levi M: I was curious, Hayley, about your initial vision of the project: uniting the youth group and bringing everyone together around a project. Do you feel it did achieve that goal? Do you feel the result of that has been positive? Have you seen that in the youth group?

Hayley D: Definitely! I think it has helped unite our youth group, especially with the number of people that ended up being involved in the album. Not only with over ten composers but also all the musicians involved. And also the album art, for example, was done by a young person. There were a lot of different areas of talent that were all involved in the album, and that was exciting as well. Gradually, throughout the year, we'd have a new song sung live by our youth group, which brought a lot of excitement.

Levi M: That's great. I think there's something to be said there for other

CYCs and youth groups where they're trying to think of something to kind of bring everyone together. Doesn't necessarily have to be an album, but having a big project like that where everyone can kind of participate in some way. The album art by Sis. Eden Dangerfield is so cool. Clearly a lot of detail and time went into putting that together.

Hayley D: And the images for the singles are zoomed-in images of the actual hand of God. So that's also another creative element that she put into it. It nicely depicts God's hand and all of His creation because God is the ultimate Creator. At the end of the day, He's also the ultimate musician. He's given us all of our musical and creative abilities. We're made in his image and can give back to Him with our talents through music. Young people have a lot of energy to give, and a lot of young people are extremely creative. I don't necessarily think our community promotes creativity as much as it could. It's vital to give creative young people avenues to channel that creativity and that energy in a healthy, positive way and give back to God the talents that he's given us.

Levi G: The point of our podcasts is to encourage more music. We hope that this story inspires people to make more music. This is such a delightful story because it is about including as many people as possible. It sounds like an encouraging process for a songwriter from the beginning, especially with people who were doing this for the first time.

Levi M: It was a great strategy to set up advisors to go to who have done it before. You've done a fantastic job of inspiring people to go out and try something. What would you say are some of the lessons you've learned throughout this process?

Hayley D: With the planning side, having a good subcommittee is important. On future projects, maybe I would suggest meeting more regularly just to discuss plans moving forward. Also, putting it to prayer, giving it to God and being patient. Having the

A group photo from one of the creating sessions.

mindset of, we are going to get this done no matter what. Giving up is not an option. Not being too perfectionistic, and remembering the ultimate aim of this is to unite our community and praise God. It's a positive thing and not something we should get too worried or stressed about.

Gideon R: I think there's a reason God has made it so enjoyable to harmonize and sing together. There's a physiological thing there. I've felt like I've almost shied away from feeling the energy when singing praise songs. But definitely, in the past couple of years, it's become more apparent in my mind that the words and the sound together are there for a purpose. It's good to feel the energy, and it's good to feel that connection to God. You know, there was a time when it didn't feel like the project would happen. Someone said this to me, I forget who it was, but they were reminiscing about the album and how it had finally come out. They were like, "Isn't it so great that even though this album was pushed back so far from when we wanted to do it, it's now getting released at a time of the highest energy at possibly one of the biggest youth conferences in Australia, and getting the widest reach and the highest possible amount of energy and praise?" And this person said that was almost like the hand of God, literally, working so much just to have the biggest impact.

Levi M: Love it. Thank you both and your entire CYC so much for your work on this album. It has benefited us personally and spiritually, and so many ecclesias worldwide will benefit from this for years to come.

Gideon R: Thank you, guys, for having us. Do you mind if I finish with a quote? This is what inspired the "Hand of God" title and the artwork.

> *Who among all these does not know that the hand of the LORD has done this? In his hand is the life of every living thing and the breath of all mankind.* (Job 12:9-10).

Levi M: That's a great way to end it. Thank you both.

Jessica Gelineau,
Simi Hills Ecclesia, CA

- You can listen to the Hand of God album on all major streaming platforms, or on the NCYC's website: https://mytidings.org/ncycmusicproject
- YouTube album link: https://mytidings.org/handofgodalbum
- Spotify link: https://mytidings.org/handofgodspotify
- Chord charts for the songs are in the process of being made available on www.ultimate-guitar.com. Search "NCYC".
- Feel free to reach out directly to Gideon or Hayley with any questions about this story, or for more chords/lyrics. hayleydanga@gmail.com or gideonryan24@gmail.com

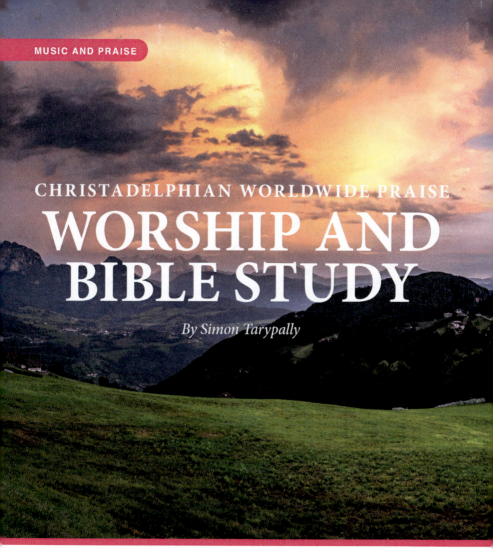

MUSIC AND PRAISE

CHRISTADELPHIAN WORLDWIDE PRAISE

WORSHIP AND BIBLE STUDY

By Simon Tarypally

SINCE 2020 Bro. Simon Tarpally has been organizing Worldwide Zoom events to facilitate the praise and worship of God. Bro. Simon was kind enough to share some of these events with us.

Christadelphian Praise and Worship Meetings

The first Christadelphian Worldwide Praise and Worship Meeting began on September 18, 2020, using the Zoom platform. This effort began during the challenging times of the global pandemic. The program is held each Friday at 5:30 PM India Standard Time (IST).

God has blessed us by providing a wonderful place to sing and rejoice with brothers and sisters. In the preliminary stages, Praise and Worship started exclusively with Indian brothers and sisters from all corners of the Indian Christadelphian ecclesias.

It was spiritually encouraging for brothers and sisters in the pandemic to connect virtually, sing hymns, and meditate on the word of God. After a few months, I posted about the Worldwide Praise and Worship Program on my Facebook profile and shared it with Christadelphian Facebook groups and worldwide ecclesias.

Gradually, the word spread through people who attended the program. Currently, the Praise and Worship Program has connected thirty-six countries. We have as many as sixty screens joining each week.

The program is about ninety minutes long and very Interactive. We start by greeting one another on Zoom with our cameras turned on and have fellowship time. We then have live praise and worship from brothers and sisters worldwide, playing musical instruments and singing hymns. This introduction is followed by speakers who provide 15-20 minutes of encouragement.

By God's grace, we have celebrated the 3rd anniversary of the Worldwide Praise and Worship meeting. We Invite all brothers and sisters to join us Weekly on Fridays at 5:30 PM India time (IST) with this Link:

Meeting ID: 846 3364 3448

Passcode: 7803621

The weekly Zoom link will remain unchanged. Other Time zones: (USA 8:00 AM EDT)/ (5:00 AM PDT) / (10:00 PM Melbourne Australia)/ (1:00 PM UK (BST).

If you would like to be added to the Mailing list and receive weekly reminders/updates and announcements, my email address is tarypally.simon@gmail.com. Also, If you would like to see and access the past Zoom recordings, please email me.

Christadelphian Worldwide Bible Study

Similarly, the second Zoom meeting and Bible study started in December 2020. This meeting is hosted weekly each Sunday at 5:00 PM IST. With brothers and sisters joining us online from 7-8, participants are spiritually encouraged. This meeting focuses on Indian brothers and sisters from places such as Kurnool, Tripura, Bangalore, Bangladesh, Chennai, Hyderabad and so on. Also, other countries, such as Bangladesh, Thailand, Myanmar, Tanzania, and Nairobi, have joined. We have finished studies on Psalms, Proverbs, Ecclesiastes, and Song of Solomon in the last two and a half years, having various international Christadelphian speakers.

Currently, we have started a new series of studies on The Prophecy of Isaiah, with speakers from the USA and Canada. You are welcome to join us on Zoom each Sunday at 5:00 pm India time (IST) with this Zoom link:

Meeting ID: 836 7189 1654

Passcode: 428057

The duration of the class is ninety minutes, using both English and Telugu word-by-word translation by myself.

We also had our first-ever India and Worldwide Christadelphian Virtual Choir Project, available on my YouTube channel and streamed on the WCF, Tidings, and ACBM websites. By releasing the Virtual Choir on January 14, 2021, we had fourteen countries and forty-three singers and musicians around the globe singing beautiful Hymn 280 ("Lift now your voice and sing"). If you want to listen to the Choir, search on YouTube for "1st India Christadelphian Virtual Choir."

The address is www.youtube.com/watch?v=KZw7iJUUtdQ

Lord willing, we are working on the second virtual choir project, which should be available soon.

So, how can you support and lend a hand?

Join us each Friday and Sunday for an uplifting praise and Bible study. You can also submit your song recordings weekly or monthly from your ecclesia by singing a hymn or your own song composition. If you are a speaker, you are most welcome to provide an address for the program. Just email me and I will add you to the schedule. Finally, if you are a brother or sister of a prayerful spirit, we have many prayer requests, and we can all pray together with one voice.

Shout for joy to God, all the earth; sing the glory of his name; give to him glorious praise!

Say to God, *"How awesome are your deeds! So great is your power that your enemies come cringing to you. All the earth worships you and sings praises to you; they sing praises to your name."* (Psa 66:1-4 ESV).

Simon Tarypally,
Hyderabad Ecclesia, India

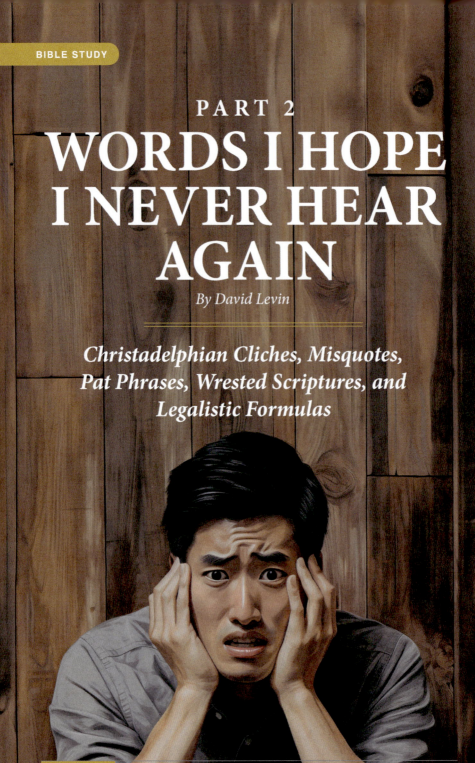

"Straight and Narrow," "In the Appointed Manner," "Pleasing in Your Sight"

THIS month, the first phrase to be dismissed forever is **"Straight and Narrow."**

What's wrong with it? It's a misunderstanding and misuse of an already misleading translation from the KJV. The main culprit is "straight," which is substituted for "strait," which properly applies to the way, not the gate. There is no "straight and narrow" in the Bible; there is a narrow gate and straight (meaning "difficult") way.

What's at stake? "Straight and narrow" is a legalistic slogan. Citing Matthew 7:13-14 to refer to our walk in Christ being "straight and narrow" promotes a stenotic religious life of "contamination avoidance" rather than developing the fruit of the spirit and a trusting relationship with God and Jesus.

How can it be fixed? Quote the verse accurately and understand what Jesus is saying: Most people lead a life of self-gratification that leads to nothingness; few people make the difficult decision of self-denial and the challenging life that leads to the Kingdom.

Discussion: Three sources of confusion contribute to corrupting this saying of Jesus, recorded only in Matthew. The first is the pair of homophones, "strait" and "straight." the second is the partially overlapping meanings of "strait" and "narrow," and the third is the KJV misapplication of "strait" to the gate and "narrow" to the way. All of this adds up to fodder for legalist minds that construe religion as an exercise in avoidance of external contamination.

Jesus' admonition to enter by the narrow gate is in the Sermon on the Mount, where he also taught that true righteousness must exceed that of the Scribes and Pharisees. The idiom "straight and narrow" aptly describes a Pharisee walking a tightrope between chasms of defilements. If "straight and narrow" were a real Bible phrase, it would be used by Jesus to describe the Pharisees, not as a guide for discipleship. It is inconceivable that Jesus was exhorting his followers to be better Pharisees, so the concept of "straight and narrow" as a prescription for religious life is dead even before examining the details.

What are the details? Jesus speaks of two gates and the roads that the gates open to. There's a narrow gate and a difficult road that leads to life, and a wide gate and easy road that leads to destruction. None of the four adjectives used to describe the gates and the roads convey any sense of "straight," meaning a direct line without bends or curves.

The KJV translators chose "strait" to describe the gate to life, presumably in the sense of "constricted," but "narrow" is the ordinary sense of that Greek word. KJV then uses "narrow" to describe the road, but "narrow" is a one-off of about 50 occurrences of the Greek adjective and its cognate noun. They are elsewhere translated as trouble, affliction, or tribulation. The root meaning is evidently something like confined or constricted, so "narrow" is understandable, but clearly Jesus was talking about a difficult road of discipleship, with its troubles and trials, not a narrow road.

Thus, the KJV adjectives "strait gate, narrow road" are reversed and misleading.

It is the gate that is narrow and the way that is strait (difficult); as translated in NIV, RSV, ESV, NKJV and others (see table).

Our way in Christ is filled with turmoil, temptations, and troubles; it is indeed a difficult road. A narrow gate makes sense too, possibly because it is hard to get through, or because it seems an unlikely entrance to anything, or because it is hard to find. Therefore, Jesus' metaphor of the narrow gate and difficult road behind it conveys that the gate to the Kingdom of God is the hard choice of giving up one's path of life to follow Jesus, and the subsequent way to eternal life will be filled with difficulties. Most people won't take that course.

The little metaphor of the narrow gate and difficult road has an important message. It's a pity that it has become the source of such a reprehensible saying as "straight and narrow."

Version	Gate to Destruction	Road to Destruction	Gate to Life	Road to Life
KJV	wide	broad	strait	narrow
RV	wide	broad	narrow	straitened
NKJV	wide	broad	narrow	difficult
RSV	wide	easy	narrow	hard
NRSV	wide	easy	narrow	hard
NIV	wide	broad	small	narrow
ESV	wide	easy	narrow	hard
NASB2000	wide	broad	narrow	constricted
Mounce	wide	easy	narrow	difficult

"In the Appointed Way"

The phrase "in the appointed way" or "in the appointed manner" is often spoken by presiders introducing the Breaking of Bread, or in prayers before taking the bread and the wine.

What's wrong with it? There is no appointed way or manner, nor is the purpose of keeping the memorial service to follow a protocol. The breaking of bread service is not a ritual we perform to satisfy God by "doing it right," as is implied by the word "appointed."

What's at stake? This is a legalistic formulation that turns the memorial service into an obligation that we fulfill rather than a ceremony introduced by Jesus to help us bring to mind his love and sacrificial life on our behalf.

How to make it better? Introduce the Breaking of Bread service by emphasizing that this is a gift from God to help us remember our Lord Jesus. Avoid any hint that we are fulfilling an obligation.

Discussion: What is meant by this phrase anyway? Is "appointed way" a Biblical term or concept? What directives are thought to be included in "appointed?" Are we following an example or making the Breaking of Bread service a duty to be performed?

The New Covenant has but two rituals: Breaking of Bread and baptism. Both of them symbolize essential aspects of the atonement. Neither one of them has any merit in the doing per se, as a good deed done to satisfy God. However, because they are rituals—that is, tangible physical acts—they can easily slide into legalistic territory.

This result is especially true of the Breaking of Bread because it is a weekly occurrence. Attendance at a meeting to break bread can become an obligation, something done to satisfy a command and invoke God's favor. The inevitable extension of a legalistic perspective on any ritual is, "There must be a right way to do it," and then the added formalities end up labeled as "the appointed way."

Remember, our community's religious worldview is influenced by what is routinely spoken on Sunday mornings or at Bible class. Partaking of the bread and wine "in the appointed way" sets the tone of fulfilling a duty, an act to satisfy God. And if we do it right, we must be righteous. A service that is meant to drive us to utter humility and appreciation of God's and Jesus' love becomes an instrument of "the salvation by works" agenda.

We are not made for the Breaking of Bread, but the Breaking of Bread is made for us. One of the presider's duties is to prepare the congregation each Sunday for that ritual of remembrance that refreshes our minds in the great act of Jesus's love for us, in his life, his teachings, and his submission to death on the cross.

> Introduce the Breaking of Bread service by emphasizing that this is a gift from God to help us remember our Lord Jesus. Avoid any hint that we are fulfilling an obligation.

"Pleasing in Your Sight"

The phrase "pleasing in your sight," or more likely, "pleasing in thy sight," is frequently included in closing prayers after a class or service.

What's wrong with it? It implies God benefits from our worship, and the purpose of Sunday morning memorial service or a Bible class is to please God and gain his favor. Also, its typical use is logically meaningless.

What's at stake? It's another legalistic encroachment, so a lot is at stake. Pleasing God is not as theologically faulty as appeasing God, but it's in the same line of thinking: that God benefits from our worship.

How can it be improved? Reverse the focus. Thank God for allowing us to join together for a service/class that has been pleasing to us.

Discussion: This legalistic formulation is conceptually similar to "in the appointed way." It implies that holding the right kind of worship service or class pleases or satisfies God–that is, God is the one who benefits. How can God benefit from our meeting together? Is the purpose of our meeting together to do something for God's sake? Who's the beneficiary of our classes, exhortation, and worship? Is God better off for what we do?

To address concern for God's pleasure leads down the same path as "in the appointed way." It emphasizes satisfying an obligation, and on doing it the right way. Even if that is not the overt intention, as soon as these words come out, they are heard by dozens or even hundreds of ears. The message is: "We do this to please God. We do it the right way." The attendees are misdirected as to the purpose of their being present.

Besides the theological travesty, closing a Sunday morning service or a Bible class by praying that what already transpired in the past hour, or two somehow pleased God makes no sense on logistical grounds. It's over; there's nothing to be done at this point. Even if it were the case that God was pleased or displeased by what had just transpired, then the prayer afterward wouldn't change a thing about God's pleasure or displeasure.

What Pleases God?

Despite the misuse of this phrase, Scripture does say that there are things that please God. There are several references to God being pleased by our behaviors. I John 3:22 is clear about this: God is pleased when we practice acts of love and faith. Hebrews 13:16 and Philippians 4:18 say that God is pleased with sacrificial acts of benevolence and generosity. When God sees you respond in a helpful way to your brothers and sisters when your faith is put to the test, then he is pleased—not because what you did benefited God, but because what you did shows that his love for you has generated a response in your heart and in your behavior. His word did not return to him void.

God is pleased when we grow spiritually. If a class or service benefitted us, then God would be pleased **for** us, not **by** us. The distinction is the difference between "pleasing God" and "pleasing to God." The former is legalistic, the performance of a required obligation, checked off and now a credit to the righteousness account. The latter is God's recognition of faith in action and spiritual growth.

God will be pleased to see that all legalistic elements are expunged from our worship proceedings, and the focus is on using the time to help us grow in our love for God and Jesus, our trust, and our development of the Fruit of the Spirit.

David Levin,
Denver Ecclesia, CO

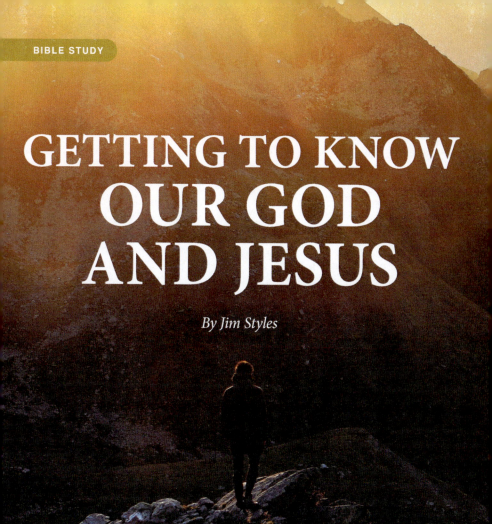

BIBLE STUDY

GETTING TO KNOW OUR GOD AND JESUS

By Jim Styles

God's Incredible Love For Us

THIS topic is one of the key first principles of our Faith, yet it took me years to realize just how essential it is that we understand and appreciate God's love. I grew up in an ecclesial atmosphere so worried about the Evangelical Revival that most members did not mention or discuss the love of God. I have witnessed many interviews for baptism that never mention God's love at all, yet God intended it to be one of the greatest motivators in our lives to battle the devil within us. Jesus said in John 17:3, *"This is eternal life, that they know you the only true God, and Jesus Christ whom you have sent."*[1] Getting to know our God and His son, Jesus, influences how we live and treat one another by providing us with the most powerful motivation to resist our natural desires and instead choose to live like our God.

Our goal every day is to come closer to the way Jesus lived. The gospels show us how Jesus treated people and make it clear that he was showing everyone the eternal way of life of his Father. As Jesus said, *"whoever has seen me has seen the Father."* (John 14:9). We do become like the God whom we worship, so we better get to know Him as the loving, merciful Father He is, and grow our relationship with Jesus Christ His son, who *"has made Him known."*

How is your relationship with Jesus Christ maturing? If he returned today, and showed up to meet you, would your reaction be one of running away in fear and trying to hide like Adam and Eve, or would you want to hug him and thank him for all he has done for you in changing your life? Do you view God as an angry Father who watches everything you do wrong and wants to punish you for all your failures, like Job's friends did? Or do you have a loving relationship with your God, seeing Him as a Father who dearly loves you, who greatly desires you to be in His family forever? He freely wants to show you mercy for your failures as you grow in His word. God sent His beloved son to engage in the battle with the devil to the end to show us how to resist Sin and trust Him. He is a Father who loves you so much He sends His angels every day to train you to understand Him so you will learn to live more like Him. Jesus put it best: *"If anyone loves me, he will keep my word, and my Father will love him, and we will come to him and make our home with him."* (John 14:23).

We sometimes think this is just a New Testament idea, but God's love for us is throughout the Bible. When the angel passed by Moses to reveal God to him, the angel proclaimed the character of God:

*The LORD, the LORD, a God merciful and gracious, slow to anger, and **abounding in steadfast love** and faithfulness, keeping **steadfast love** for thousands, forgiving iniquity and transgression and sin, but who will by no means clear the guilty.* (Exod 34:6-7).

Moses reminded the people that they were:

*a holy people to the Lord your God; the LORD your God has chosen you to be a people for Himself... **because the Lord loves you**, and because He would keep the oath which He swore to your fathers* (Deut 7:6-8 NKJV).

God hoped that if His people understood and appreciated His love for them, they would respond by showing God's love to others. They should have learned to treat others with the same love, kindness, patience, compassion and mercy that motivated God in His treatment of His people— and so should we! Deuteronomy 10:12-20 reminds us,

The LORD set his heart in love on your fathers and chose their offspring after them... He executes justice for the fatherless and the widow, and loves the sojourner, giving him food and clothing. Love the sojourner, therefore, for you were sojourners in the land of Egypt.

When we experience and appreciate God's love towards us and recognize how He is doing so much every day to train and save us, it motivates us to show others the same love, mercy and patience. This changes our lives, how we interact with people, and our willingness to show love, compassion and mercy to others who sometimes fail in the battle with sin, just like us.

Our God has always been motivated by His love for us. Still, He expects that His love, mercy and patience will drive us to fight sin in our lives as Paul reminded us:

Or do you presume on the riches of his kindness and forbearance and patience, not knowing that God's kindness is meant to lead you to repentance? (Rom 2:4).

God's love for us is not unconditional! He expects us to respond by changing our lives to be more like His. We sometimes forget one of the great blessings in the promises to Abraham was that God would motivate people to resist Sin. As Peter proclaims:

You are the sons of the prophets and of the covenant that God made with your fathers, saying to Abraham, 'And in your offspring shall all the families of the earth be blessed.' God, having raised up his servant, sent him to you first, **to bless you by turning every one of you from your wickedness.** *(Acts 3:25-26).*

God does expect us to develop into His children, reveal His love, and learn to live His eternal way of life if we hope to join His family forever.

Although we may begin our relationship with God based on our fear of God disciplining us for all our failures, God hopes our relationship with Him will mature **to become based on love, not fear**. It's like a two-year-old child learning not to walk out into a busy street because they may fear the discipline they will receive, as opposed to that same child as a teenager who accepts and trusts their parents' guidance because they love their parents, not because they fear some discipline that may follow.

Love has so much more power to change our lives for good, than fear. Remember when Joseph's brothers made up the story about the wild animal killing Joseph because they feared telling Jacob the truth? Yars later when Judah pleaded with Joseph to take Benjamin's place, it was because Judah loved Jacob and could not bear to see Jacob deal with the loss of another son. Or as John puts it in 1 John 4:18, *"There is no fear in love, but perfect love casts out fear. For fear has to do with punishment, and whoever fears has not been perfected in love."* God knows He cannot give eternal life to those who primarily serve Him because they fear punishment. Once they were given immortality, their main motivation to serve would be gone! But if we are motivated by love, God knows that this will drive us to serve Him and love His family forever, because *"love never ends"* and *"the greatest of these is love."* (1 Cor 13).

God didn't wait until we were spiritually developed and worth saving to redeem us. He didn't hold out until we asked for forgiveness and mercy. His love for us drove Him to initiate a plan and carry it out so he could save us by his grace despite our ungodliness and sinfulness. Even though we:

> All once lived in the passions of our flesh, carrying out the desires of the body and mind...But God, being rich in mercy, **because of the great love with which he loved us**, even when we were dead in our trespasses, made us alive together with Christ by grace you have been saved–and raised us up with him and seated us with him in the heavenly places in Christ Jesus. (Eph 2:3-6).

An accurate understanding and appreciation of how God loves and acts should compel us to become more like Him in treating others when they spiritually fail. We must become more like our God and take the first step in seeking to save those who have missed the mark, provide a pathway for them to be restored in mercy and grace, and then prayerfully do our best to help and support their journey. Paul reminds us all that,

> When **we were still without strength**, in due time [at just the right time (NIV)] Christ died for the **ungodly**. For scarcely for a righteous man will one die; yet perhaps for a good man someone would even dare to die. But God demonstrates His own love toward us, in that while we were still **sinners**, Christ died for us. (Rom 5:6-8 NKJV).

God's love was real, planned for over 4,000 years, and it cost Him, and it was all for humans who did not deserve it! The Bible makes it clear in the lives of Jacob, Samson, David, the woman caught in adultery, Peter, and so many others that our God does not want to condemn us for our sins and mistakes. Still, He is very interested in what we learn from them and if we are growing in faith. God hopes that, like the woman caught in the act of adultery, we will *"sin no more."*

There are times when God's love for us causes Him to bring sad, devastating events into our lives or the lives of others to cause us to consider our ways or to demonstrate and grow our faith and trust in God. As God reminded His people through Isaiah, *"I form light and create darkness, I make well-being and create calamity, I am the Lord, who does all these things."* (Isa 45:6). Just as any Dad or Mom today must discipline a child, they love to train them, so our loving Father must discipline us through the experiences of life so we will mature into His children, learning to live His eternal way of life. We can completely trust that when God chastens us, *"God is treating you as sons"* and *"He disciplines us for our good, that we may share his holiness."* (Heb 12:7,10).

We must communicate to our children, grandchildren, and interested friends the love God has for all of us and that everything He does in our lives is done in love, for our good, because He greatly desires us to become members of His eternal family. We can confidently trust that whatever illnesses, accidents, financial troubles,

family problems and ecclesial issues that God causes to surface in our lives, He is in control, working for our good to train us to become His children who live like the loving Father who *"of his own will he brought us forth by the word of truth, that we should be a kind of first fruits of his creatures."* (Jas 1:18). It's not easy to change us, with our nature so prone to sin, into children of God, but our loving Father has taken on that challenge and *"I am sure of this, that he who began a good work in you will bring it to completion at the day of Jesus Christ."* (Phil 1:6).

What a privilege we have today to have been called by God into His family. *"See what kind of love the Father has given to us, that we should be called children of God; and so we are."* (1 John 3:1). Getting to know the love God has for us, that same love He revealed in the life of Jesus, will energize us with a motivating power to change the way we live. Let's respond to His love by keeping His commandments and loving one another with the kind of love God shows us every day. As John reminds us:

Beloved, let us love one another, for love is from God, and whoever loves has been born of God and knows God. Anyone who does not love does not know God, because God is love. (1 John 4:7-8).

Jim Styles,
Simi Hills Ecclesia, CA

---

1 All Scriptural citations are taken from the New King James Version, unless specifically noted.

FIRST PRINCIPLES

PREACHING THE FIRST PRINCIPLES IN A POST-CHRISTIAN WORLD

By Richard Morgan

WE live in a post-Christian world. More and more people identify themselves as atheist or agnostic. Even if someone claims to believe in some kind of higher spiritual power, many are functional atheists, having no semblance of a relationship with that higher power. Other people are turning away from Christianity to become "spiritual" or to embrace Eastern religion. Church attendance has been declining for decades, and our preaching efforts often prove fruitless.

How do we preach the first principles of the doctrine of God in such a post-Christian world? Mention the Bible, or the God of the Bible, Jesus, or quote Bible passages, and you're met with blank stares. It can be a frustrating venture to try to tell people about our hope when we are met with the Biblically illiterate masses.

Thankfully, we have direction in Scripture to guide our efforts. The first-century world was not so different from ours. In Judea, there were plenty of Jews, but few of them understood their true Messiah and what the Hope of Israel means. Outside of Judea, most people knew nothing of Yahweh, the God of the Bible. But that did not stop the Lord Jesus Christ, who, having been raised from the dead, appeared to Saul of Tarsus on the road to Damascus. He gave his new apostle the following commission:

But rise and stand upon your feet, for I have appeared to you for this purpose, to appoint you as a servant and witness to the things in which you have seen me and to those in which I will appear to you, delivering you from your people and from the Gentiles—to whom I am sending you to open their eyes, so that they may turn from darkness to light and from the power of Satan to God, that they may receive forgiveness of sins and a place among those who are sanctified by faith in me. (Acts 26:16-18).

Saul of Tarsus would be sent to the Gentiles, a people who did not know Yahweh. They were, as verse 18 says, "*in darkness,*" and Saul's mission was to open their eyes just as his eyes were opened so that he might turn from the blinkered form of Judaism he formerly embraced.

When he went on his first missionary journey through the Gentile world, one of his first ports of call was the synagogue in Pisidian Antioch. His first recorded speech, delivered to the Jews, however, was met with antagonism. Curiously, the eyes of the Jews were just as blind as the Gentiles. So Paul, as he was now known in Gentile lands, told the Jews "*Since you thrust it aside and judge yourselves unworthy of eternal life, behold, we are turning to the Gentiles.*" (Acts 13:46). He then referred to his commission by quoting the prophet Isaiah:

For so the Lord has commanded us, saying, "I have made you a light for the Gentiles, that you may bring salvation to the ends of the earth." (Acts 13:47).

We'll come back to this quotation in a moment, but first think back to Saul's conversion. He did begin preaching right away, but it quickly became obvious he was too green, and he was sent back to Tarsus for between three and nine years or more (Acts 9:26-28).

What do you suppose Paul did while he was back in his hometown for so many years? Jesus had given him an enormously difficult task: to preach the gospel message to a Biblically illiterate people steeped in all kinds of philosophies and idolatry.

I think there's a clue as to what he was doing in his use of that quotation from Isaiah. The words are found in two places in the prophetic record—Isaiah 42:6 and 49:6. The passage in chapter 49 speaks of someone called *"from the womb"* (v. 1), as was the apostle Paul (Gal 1:15). The next verse (Isa 49:2) says *"He made my mouth like a sharp sword,"* pointing to Paul being a preacher to the Gentiles (Gal 1:16).

But it's the passage in Isaiah 42 which is more significant for the Apostle Paul because it mentions the commission he had received on the road to Damascus: to open the blind eyes of the Gentiles and bring them out of darkness:

> *I am the LORD; I have called you in righteousness; I will take you by the hand and keep you; I will give you as a covenant for the people, a light for the nations, to open the eyes that are blind, to bring out the prisoners from the dungeon, from the prison those who sit in darkness.* (Isa 42:6-7).

Paul had been taken by the hand (Acts 9:8) after being made blind so that he might see. And now he was going to pass on that experience to the Gentiles. So, as we can tell from the quotes in Acts 13, both passages would have been very meaningful for Paul. That is especially so because of the wider context. Remember, he was to preach to a world full of idolatry. At this he was successful—*"you turned to God from idols to serve the living and true God."* (1 Thess 1:9). And the prophecy of Isaiah would prove the backbone for his preaching because Isaiah 40-55 contains a series of polemics against idolatry. For instance, the next verse in Isaiah 42 says:

> *I am the LORD; that is my name; my glory I give to no other, nor my praise to carved idols.* (Isa 42:8).

These chapters in Isaiah teach one of the most basic first principle doctrines of all—there is only one God, His name is Yahweh, and all other gods are the figments of people's imaginations. What better passage of Scripture for Paul to pour over during his time in Tarsus? And we know he did study Isaiah because of the amount of time he spent quoting it in his epistles to the Gentile ecclesias, particularly in Romans, 1 Corinthians, and Galatians.

Along with Isaiah, there is one other main passage Paul must have studied while in Tarsus. It is a chapter in Deuteronomy that forms the background of Isaiah 44 and teaches about the folly of idols (vv. 9-10). Isaiah 44 begins with these words:

> *But now hear, O Jacob my servant, Israel whom I have chosen! Thus says the LORD who made you, who formed you from the womb and will help you: Fear not, O Jacob my servant, Jeshurun whom I have chosen.* (Isa 44:1-2).

We have an echo here of chapter 49 with the mention of God's servant being *"formed from the womb."* And, while both passages apply initially to

> "I am the first and I am the last; besides me there is no god. Who is like me? Let him proclaim it. Let him declare and set it before me, since I appointed an ancient people. Let them declare what is to come, and what will happen. Fear not, nor be afraid; have I not told you from of old and declared it? And you are my witnesses! Is there a God besides me?"

Israel, they also point forward to Paul as the Apostle of the Gentiles, just as the Jews would be witnesses to the God of Israel among the nations.

But it's the nickname for Israel, Jeshurun (v. 2), which tells us that this passage is based on Deuteronomy. It is a name only found here in Isaiah 44, Deuteronomy 32:15, and 33:5.

Isaiah 44 contains symbolic language of preaching among the Gentiles before we come to the following:

> *Thus says the LORD, the King of Israel and his Redeemer, the LORD of hosts: "I am the first and I am the last; besides me there is no god. Who is like me? Let him proclaim it. Let him declare and set it before me, since I appointed an ancient people. Let them declare what is to come, and what will happen. Fear not, nor be afraid; have I not told you from of old and declared it? And you are my witnesses! Is there a God besides me?"* (Isa 44:6-8).

These are some of those typical words of Isaiah outlining the basic doctrine of the oneness and incomparability of Yahweh. There is further evidence that it's based on Deuteronomy 32 by using the word translated *"God"* in verse 8, which is not the normal word *elohim* but the much rarer *eloah*. This instance is the only time Isaiah uses this word in his prophecy, but the first two occurrences (and the only occurrences in the Pentateuch) are in Deuteronomy 32 (in bold below):

> *But Jeshurun grew fat, and kicked; you grew fat, stout, and sleek; then he forsook **God** who made him and scoffed at the Rock of his salvation. They stirred him to jealousy with strange gods; with abominations they provoked him to anger. They sacrificed to demons that were no gods, to **gods** they had never known, to new gods that had come recently, whom your fathers had never dreaded.* (Deut 32:15-17).

As you can see from these verses, Deuteronomy 32 is a polemic against idolatry (here, the idolatry Israel would fall into by flirting with the Gentile nations), forming a fitting background for Isaiah. In the chapter, God describes himself as a rock (vv. 4, 15, 18, 30-31), which Isaiah calls God in Isa. 44:8—*"Is there a God besides me? There is no Rock; I know not any."*

Deuteronomy 32:39 sums up the incomparability of Yahweh with: *"See now that I, even I, am he, and there is* no god beside me." The key phrase *"I am he"* is used for God in several similar passages in Isaiah 41:4; 43:10, 13; 46:4; 48:12. That same verse in Deuteronomy continues with the words *"I kill and I make alive; I wound and I heal,"* which accord with Isaiah 45:

> I am the LORD, and there is no other, besides me there is no God; I equip you, though you do not know me, that people may know, from the rising of the sun and from the west, that there is none besides me; I am the LORD, and there is no other. I form light and create darkness; I make well-being and create calamity; I am the LORD, who does all these things. (Isa 45:5-7).

Deuteronomy 32 also tells us that God is interested in all nations:

> When the Most High gave to the nations their inheritance, when he divided mankind, he fixed the borders of the peoples according to the number of the sons of God. But the LORD's portion is his people, Jacob his allotted heritage. (Deut 32:8-9).

Since *"the Most High gave to the nations their inheritance,"* we understand Yahweh is completely sovereign in all the earth. Ultimately, He is the God of the Gentiles, even though they didn't know it.

When talking about the gospel going out to the Gentiles, Paul quoted verse 43 of the same chapter in Romans 15:10. However, he clearly used the Septuagint rendering, which reads, *"Delight, O nations, with his people."*

Deuteronomy 32, therefore, forms the basis of Isaiah's preaching about the unity of God and diatribes against idolatry. The chapter, along with Isaiah, are some of the stock passages Paul used in his preaching efforts to the Gentiles.

We live in a similar world to Paul's, a world full of idolatry, antagonistic to the idea of the one true God of Israel. The idols we encounter differ from those in the first century. They are more subtle but just as potently capable of enslaving people to false religion, even those who subscribe to atheism. The example of Paul and his use of Isaiah and Deuteronomy 32 can guide us as we attempt to preach the gospel message in a world full of darkness. In this series, we shall examine Paul's example by focusing on his speech in a hotbed of worldly philosophy—Athens. There, we shall see Paul build bridges, establish common ground, and through the power of Scripture—even without quoting it to the Biblically illiterate—convince at least some of his listeners to turn from idols to serve the living and true God.

Richard Morgan,
Simi Hills Ecclesia, CA

BOOK REVIEW

STARTERS

Written by Bruce Parker
Reviewed by Mike Hardy

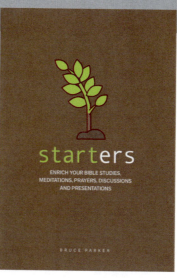

STARTERS consists, as the title says, of fifty-two ideas that act as a starting point for talks, sermons, discussions, and private study. It is the intention of the writer and of the publisher that they will reach a wider readership than our community, so the content lacks a particularly Christadelphian "flavor." Each chapter is short enough not to be prescriptive and long enough to provide sufficient material for development. They avoid the danger of predictability, remaining lively, inventive and enjoyable.

The topics are organized under the headings: Christian Walk, Relationships, Bible, God and Jesus, Trials and Faith. The appendix gives examples where the framework has been worked up into a complete presentation.

William Barclay wrote that the success of a talk depended on three things: "You must give your listeners something to learn, something to feel and something to do." We are good at "something to learn." Most of our talks are consistently Bible-based. One of the virtues of this book is that it also addresses the other two categories. Unless the "something to learn" generates an emotional response in us, it remains an academic exercise, and we can keep at arms' length any implication that we need to make a change in our life. The need for "something to feel' is addressed in the book by suggestions for further prayer and meditation. *Starters* is also an intensely practical book with suggestions for further action: "something to do."

Bro. Parker writes that "The aim is that the studies will draw the listener to Christ, to loving service, to a fresh love of God's word." Personally, I have found the book most useful in private study, leading and challenging my thoughts and providing encouragement for my own Christian walk.

Mike Hardy,
Kindal Ecclesia, UK

NEW PRAISE BOOK

We are excited to announce that a new volume of around 130 original songs composed by Christadelphians, is launching in April 2024, Lord Willing. This third book will have a blue cover. You might remember the purple Worship Book from 2008, and orange Worship Book from 2016. Like our previous volumes, this collection will consist of original praise songs for personal and congregational worship and solo and choral items. We are excited that this volume contains works by new composers and lyricists from our current youth who have grown up with the Worship Book as part of their standard praise repertoire. Like previous volumes, we anticipate hard copies will sell out. Digital books are still available for purple and orange books, and will also be available for the blue book. To pre-order your book, please go to **www.theworshipbook.com**. Pre-orders help us determine how many books to print.

Rachel Hocking,
Kedron Brook Ecclesia, QL

TEACHING AND PREACHING

GOOD MORNING VIETNAM!

By Alan Ghent

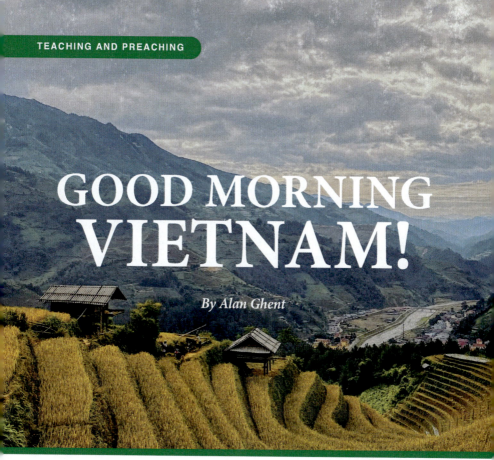

THE call sign of a US Army radio broadcaster in Saigon during the Vietnam War sadly did not bring a "Good Morning" to this war-torn nation. The communist victory resulted in many South Vietnamese fleeing the country, often by boat, searching for more hospitable shores.

One of these vessels ran aground in Indonesia and ended up in Australia, where a remarkable story began to unfold for a young Vietnamese teenager. A kind-hearted Christadelphian introduced Onesiphorus (a pseudonym for security reasons) to the gospel. While the two waited for a bus, he shared his Hope. He then talked of the Truth while in transit, sharing his seat with his young student. Later, after his baptism, Bro. Onesiphorus took to heart the Great Commission to share the Good News in his native country.

Just as Bezaleel and Aholiab were equipped with unique skills to construct the Tabernacle, providentially, this brother was equipped to build the Body of Christ in Vietnam. His business and sports abilities enabled him to make many connections with important decision-makers.

For several reasons, preaching the gospel here is a daunting proposition. Here are some of the challenges faced in Vietnam.

- Our members are not a recognized denomination. Fearful of social unrest, the government has cast a broad net to quash any movement that could destabilize the country. Although Christadelphians are no threat, unrecognized Christian groups have come under heavy scrutiny, and consequently, our preaching efforts must remain under the radar. Numerous Vietnamese brothers and sisters have been arrested, beaten, and jailed for their allegiance to the Lord Jesus Christ. At the time of writing, a recent crackdown has resulted in the suspension of Sunday services in the delta, and a brother presently remains under house arrest.
- The country is steeped in Buddhist culture. The words of Isaiah come to mind: *"For, behold, darkness covers the earth, and thick darkness is over the peoples."* (Isa 60:2 BSB). Preaching the truth as it is in Jesus is seen as an unwelcome challenge to the status quo.
- There is a language barrier with English, only sporadically spoken in the large urban centers. On a brighter note, English instruction is now mandatory in schools because the government seeks stronger economic ties with the West. Although Bro. Onesiphorus is bilingual, North American visitors are at a distinct disadvantage in sharing their Hope in their native tongue. All teaching is done in Vietnamese.

The growth of the brotherhood in Vietnam is an untold story. To safeguard the brothers and sisters, no personal names or photos are included. Currently, there are eight ecclesias and over three hundred brothers and sisters. The Asia-Pacific Christadelphian Bible Mission (ACBM) is the primary support for Vietnam. A Williamsburg Christadelphian Foundation (WCF) team recently visited four ecclesias in the southern delta region and the Ho Chi Minh City (HCMC) base of operations. This city serves as the meeting place of the HCMC Ecclesia, and as a hostel for brothers and sisters who require medical treatment in an urban center. An array of literature translated into Vietnamese can be found here, including a Sunday School syllabus. Providentially, these materials have received governmental endorsement.

On arriving at a rural ecclesia in the delta for lunch, an assortment of footwear was left at the threshold (pictured on the next page). The instruction to Moses at the burning bush came to mind: *"Take your sandals off your feet, for the place where you stand is holy ground."* (Exod 3:5 NKJV). The facility was indeed set apart for God. A caretaker couple calls it home during the week. Still, with extra washrooms and a large commercially sized kitchen, it serves as an ideal ecclesial meeting place, away from prying eyes. It is also holy in another sense, in that Christ is present when brothers and sisters meet and reflect his character. We were touched by the warm fraternal hospitality of the ecclesia members, who took a day off from their work or school to welcome us.

Footwear outside the ecclesial hall

These ecclesial facilities were generously purchased and donated to the members of Vietnam. The ecclesias were also equipped with the means to earn a livelihood. We visited three cottage industries near the meeting places—a pork farm with an adjacent rice paddy field, a shrimp pond, and charcoal kilns to provide fuel for domestic cooking. These activities grant brethren an essential livelihood while providing dignity and a sense of self-worth.

An invitation to lunch and Bible study at another rural ecclesia had to be cut short because of a visit by an inquisitive local authority, ostensibly arriving to sell lottery tickets. The appearance of Westerners off the beaten track had attracted attention in the local village. Our Bible study was canceled, and we simply became Westerners out to sample a rural lunch. As we were leaving the ecclesia, an afternoon propaganda broadcast echoed across the fields from loudspeakers, encouraging the farmers to be more productive. Indeed, the fields are ripe for harvest—but of a different sort.

The rapid growth of the Truth in Vietnam is due, in part, to seeds planted by Indigenous White Fields workers—local missionaries who use the touch-to-teach model of the Lord Jesus, which addresses both material and spiritual needs. A dozen brethren receive a small stipend and the use of a scooter to preach. They provide pastoral support and serve their local communities. These workers know the lay of the land, the language, and the culture. This advantage offers a continuing presence in their communities without drawing attention to themselves. These are skills and knowledge that Westerners lack.

On Sunday morning, we remembered Christ's sacrifice at a hotel in an urban center in the Mekong Delta. The hotel is owned by a Christian of a "recognized" denomination, who was not afraid to rent us a room. This venue enabled brethren from the local ecclesias to join for worship. We arrived and departed two or three at a time to avoid attracting attention. One side of the room was shoehorned full of Sunday School students, and the other was full of brothers and sisters sitting on the floor while the more senior members took seats on the beds. The heat hopelessly overpowered the air conditioners and fans, so the windows were open to catch the breeze. Our guardian angels kept us safe as the English exhortations translated into Vietnamese drifted down to the street. Hymns were read, rather than sung, and our service ended without a feared knock on the door by the authorities.

What Can We Do?

What can we do to further the effort in Vietnam? Without the ability to navigate the political landscape, the presence of North Americans would be a liability, and any attempts at public preaching would result in prompt incarceration. We can, however, pray for God to give the increase and to encamp his angels about our Vietnamese brethren and deliver them from persecution.

We can also help materially. In Romans 15, Paul stresses the importance of reciprocity—the practice of exchanging things with others for mutual benefit. Because the Gentiles had benefited from the Jews' rich spiritual heritage, the Gentiles were to respond by offering to the Jews what they had in abundance, namely their material resources. How does this apply to our brethren in Vietnam and the developing world? Looking at our aging Christadelphian demographics in North America, we can be encouraged by the growth of the Truth elsewhere in the world, beyond the malaise of our Western post-Christian humanist culture. We will pass our baton to these younger, faithful brothers and sisters in the developing world. They offer us a growth trajectory; we can offer them our material blessings, which we have in relative abundance. Contributions may be made through the ACBM or the WCF.

The needs in Vietnam are considerable. Most brethren in the Delta live a life of subsistence. They remain dependent upon outside support for healthcare. In times of crisis—drought, typhoon, or pandemic there are no personal reserves to fall back on. During the recent pandemic, many of these brethren who work as subsistence farmers were confined to their homes and could not plant or tend their crops. This situation provides an opportunity to fulfill the Biblical mandate to care for the poor in practical ways and steward the resources God has given us. Dental decay is rampant and is sadly characteristic of many Sunday School students. Our Lord held a special affection for these little ones, and so can we.

In addition to physical needs, there are also ongoing spiritual needs. Bibles we take for granted must be purchased from a recognized denomination, and each copy registered. A leaders' study planned for next year will require the added expense of safety measures—

A bedroom for members needing healthcare in HCMC

[The situation in Vietnam] provides an opportunity to fulfill the Biblical mandate to care for the poor in practical ways and steward the resources God has given us.

considerations that in North America are unnecessary.

The Sun of Righteousness

One day, the phrase, "Good Morning Vietnam!" will ring true. The Sun of Righteousness will appear with healing in his beams to begin the work of restoring the earth as it was originally intended. And the Vietnamese brothers and sisters, together with all nations, will benefit from a new world order of peace and righteousness. It will be a world where brothers and sisters from the four corners of the globe will constitute that great apocryphal multitude and will stand *"before the throne and before the Lamb, clothed in white robes, with palm branches in their hands… crying out with a loud voice, 'Salvation belongs to our God who sits on the throne, and to the Lamb!'"*(Rev 7:9, 10 ESV). But Christ has not yet returned, so our window of opportunity remains to express our gratitude for all that the Lord Jesus has done for us. Your prayers, your participation, and your financial support.

Alan Ghent,
North Toronto Ecclesia, ON

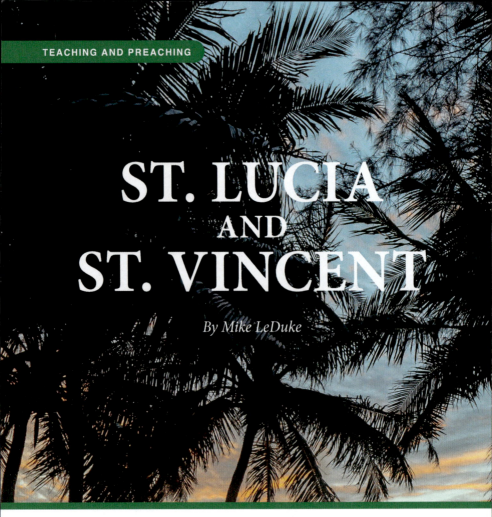

TEACHING AND PREACHING

ST. LUCIA AND ST. VINCENT

By Mike LeDuke

ALTHOUGH there is ongoing work with the St. Lucia Ecclesia while missionaries are absent via ZOOM for Sunday morning meetings and Tuesday morning Bible Classes, there is no substitute for the face-to-face fellowship and connection to the wider Christadelphian community provided by visiting Mission workers.

Bro. Martin and Sis. Lois Webster visited the island from mid-January to mid-February. I followed up with a visit from the beginning of March to mid-April. God willing, I will be there again from June 21 to July 28 and perhaps a while longer should there be a need to extend the visit.

During these visits, we have regular Sunday morning meetings, Bible Classes for the Ecclesia, and numerous ongoing classes with contacts. At the end of March, these classes bore fruit as we witnessed the first baptism in St. Lucia since before the pandemic.

On Tuesday afternoon, March 28, Julian Jackson, a contact of many years, was baptized. On April 2, he was welcomed into fellowship.

I plan to make a return visit in June-July to try to keep the momentum going, as other contacts in St. Lucia are "not far from the Kingdom of God," and whom, God willing, we may bring into our circle of fellowship through the waters of baptism.

St. Vincent and the Grenadines

On another front, I am using the contact information obtained through www.thisisyourbible.com to assess the utility of visiting St. Vincent and the Grenadines soon (perhaps in November) in conjunction with another visit to St. Lucia. Providentially, a direct flight service from St. Lucia to St. Vincent has begun earlier this year. The flight is only 30 minutes one-way. Before this, the only route to St. Vincent from St. Lucia was via either Barbados or Trinidad.

A real plus to this new service is that the flight originates from the Castries municipal airport and not from the main international airport, a 2-hour drive to the island's south end. Castries airport is less than a 10-minute taxi ride from the Mission House!

As of June 12, there are 135 contacts registered on www.thisisyourbible.com from St. Vincent. This development makes the prospect for useful work there seem very promising indeed! Through the system, I can set up a mass mailing to all of our St. Vincent contacts urging them to attend a special effort in Kingstown, St. Vincent. If you would like me to do that for the contacts in your area, just let me know. My email address is mduke@gto.net.

Please keep our little Ecclesia in Castries, St. Lucia, in your prayers. Both for the continued spread of the Gospel there and for the welfare of your brothers and sisters who remain faithful under trying conditions.

Mike LeDuke,
Cambridge Ecclesia, ON
Link Brother for St. Lucia
and St. Vincent

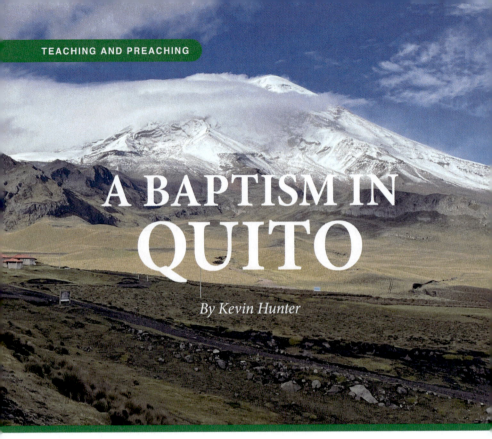

TEACHING AND PREACHING

A BAPTISM IN QUITO

By Kevin Hunter

MY company gives its employees the week of July 4th off, and this year my kids had other plans (the temerity!) So they gently cajoled me to find my own friends and activities, which allowed me to drop down to Ecuador for a week. Bro. Ruben Barboza from Cordoba, Argentina, also had some flexibility that week and agreed to fly up to meet with me.

We visited, saw most of the brothers and sisters, and did a few other things.

On the first Saturday afternoon, we hosted a "panoramic view of the Bible" for members and interested friends, as we had several out-of-towners and first-timers. We spent the afternoon starting from Genesis to integrate all our various doctrines and beliefs into a broader coherent narrative. We had good participation from everyone.

On Sunday, we held the memorial service meeting in person at the hotel we've used for the last five or six years, and had a pretty solid group attend, including a few new visitors. For the lecture/study, we broke into groups and did a deep dive into the women in Matthew 1 (the reading for that day), with each group presenting their conclusions at the end.

For most of the week, Ruben and I traveled around Quito, having 2–3-hour meetings with the brothers and sisters. Bro. Rodrigo, the de facto recording brother, was recently laid off and is looking for other work or options. He probably had the longest/toughest brush with COVID of anyone who didn't succumb (20 days on respirator), and the last few years have been rough. But he's focused now on pulling the ecclesia together and doing what we can. He is married to Sis. Jeanneth, daughter of Bro. and Sis. Galo & Ana.

One evening, Sis. Fabiola and I interviewed Rosa Duchi, Bro. Manuel's second daughter. She came through the SS and CYC while we were there in 2003-2008 and then was mostly disconnected from us for about a decade before returning more recently. She was baptized that afternoon. The Duchi's are a large family, and God willing this baptism will be the start of the second and third generations committing to Christ.

On Wednesday, we went down to Ambato with Bre. Diego and Fredy and visited with Bro. Vinicio and his family, and on Thursday morning, we climbed Carihuairazo (16,000 feet) with Vinicio and his son before returning that evening.

The two largest families in Quito (descendants and family of Bro. & Sis Galo & Ana and Sis. Clemencia) are now meeting regularly in person. God willing, we are exploring getting a hall again, likely on the north end of Quito, where about 85% of the members are. They are moving cautiously but ideally, they would find something in the Fall. After many years of ecclesial fragmentation and COVID, this is very encouraging.

The first group in Quito was baptized twenty years ago this Fall. At the time, most of them were close to retirement, meaning the group is now anywhere from 75 to 90 years old. We saw them all during this visit, but meeting in person is challenging.

Kevin Hunter,
San Diego Ecclesia, WA
Link Brother for Ecuador

THE CHRISTADELPHIAN
TIDINGS
OF THE KINGDOM OF GOD

is published monthly, except bimonthly in July-August, by The **Christadelphian Tidings**, 567 Astorian Drive, Simi Valley, CA 93065-5941.

FIRST CLASS POSTAGE PAID at Simi Valley, CA and at additional mailing offices. POSTMASTER: Send address changes to The Christadelphian Tidings, 567 Astorian Dr., Simi Valley, CA 93065.

Christadelphian Tidings Publishing Committee: Alan Markwith (Chairman), Joe Hill, John Bilello, Peter Bilello, Linda Beckerson, Nancy Brinkerhoff, Shawn Moynihan, Kevin Flatley, Jeff Gelineau, William Link, and Ken Sommerville.

Christadelphian Tidings Editorial Committee: Dave Jennings (Editor), Section Editors: Nathan Badger (Life Application), TBA (Exhortation and Consolation), Jessica Gelineau (Music and Praise), Steve Cheetham (Exposition), Richard Morgan (First Principles), Dave Jennings (Teaching and Preaching), Jan Berneau (CBMA/C), George Booker, (Thoughts on the Way, Q&A), John Bilello (Letters to the Editor), Jeff Gelineau (News and Notices, Subscriptions), Melinda Flatley (Writer Recruitment and Final Copy), and Shawn Moynihan (Books).

Subscriptions: The Tidings Magazine is provided **FREE** for any who would like to read it. The Magazine is available in PDF Format online at **tidings.org**. If you would like to order a printed subscription to **The Tidings** you may do so simply by making a donation to cover the printing costs. The Suggested Donation for printing and shipping is **USD $70.00;** (we ask for a Minimum Donation of USD $35.00 for a printed subscription.)

All subscription information is available online at **www.tidings.org**. You may subscribe online and make donations online or by mail to the above address. Information on how to subscribe in other countires is also available online at **www.tidings.org/subscribe**.

The Christadelphian Tidings is published on the 15th of the month for the month following. Items for publication must be received by the 1st of the month. Correspondence to the editor, Dave Jennings at **editor@tidings.org**. Publication of articles does not presume editorial endorsement except on matters of fundamental doctrine as set forth in the BASF. Letters should be sent via e-mail to **letters@tidings.org**. Please include your name, address and phone number. The magazine reserves the right to edit all submissions for length and clarity.

©2023, Tidings Publishing Committee. In the spirit of Christ ask for permission before reproducing any material. Contact us at **editor@tidings.org**